Mastering Decentralized Finance (DeFi)

UNDERSTAND DEFI, DESTROY FEAR OF BANKRUPTCY AFTER CRYPTO REVOLUTION AND INVEST FOR A BETTER FUTURE

ZACH GILDON

The Future is DeFi, Stop Living in the Past!

If you've not yet transitioned to the decentralized world, you're living in the past! Don't be surprised when you see more crypto millionaires rising by the day. There's more where they're coming from, considering the diversity and size of this industry, as covered in this book. You're leaving a lot on the table by not making use of this system. In order to make remarkable strides in your finances, you've got to follow smart money!

The traditional banking system is fraudulent, and it has exploited you for a long time now. You have to ask yourself if your financial service provider is making you money or you're making money for them. From stringent protocols that make the way you access your funds a pain, to dipping heavily into your honeypot, banks have been and continue to be bullies in the financial sector. Despite the 2008 crisis that proved that they can't be trusted, these poor service providers continue squeezing you for every penny, mainly because they know that your options are limited.

But woe unto them! For you have stumbled onto a gem. A disruptive beast and the biggest threat to centralized financial service providers! Two words, Decentralized Finance! Or DeFi for short. Accessing your money has never been this flexible! I mean, borderless, transparent, permissionless, interoperable, and user-friendliness! You work hard for your money, and what you choose to do with it, is your business. DeFi has come to your rescue!

Mastering Decentralized Finance (DeFi) is a book that will not only give you basics on cryptocurrencies and their dynamics, but also your compass in your journey to gain full control of your money. Better investment opportunities can be realized through decentralized autonomous organizations (DAOs), and emerging DeFi categories and markets. In this book you will learn the following:

- Mastering blockchain technology with DeFi
- Decentralized applications and DAOs that will go mainstream

- A guide to tokenized derivatives you should take advantage of
- Best liquidity pools and best farms with great annual percentage yield (APY) and solid fundamentals
- Risks involved and how to navigate around them for optimum returns

Through the informative investors' guide to this digital gold, you will get full guidance on the best yield farms to profit from, on becoming liquidity providers, and on accessing flash loans with no credit score or any form of identification. Not only that, but you will also know the trending financial projects with great potential, such as the reason behind the non-fungible token (NFT) craze as well as the dynamic future presented by the metaverse and Web 3.0 developments.

You will have insightful access to the game changers to invest in while they are in their infancy stage. If you want an easy understanding of this once complex subject, or at least how they want you to perceive it, plunge into the depths of this material head first. Learn sustainable ways of making money in this eon and avoid substantial losses!

FREE GOODIES FOR OUR DEAR READERS

Congratulations!

You are eligible for free coloring books, self-organizing planner and many more gifts.Get Free Goodies, free books and many more surprises by connecting with us.

Just email us at: info@hafizpublications.com

Or Visit us at hafizpublications.com

Table of Contents

Introduction

It's no secret that for years we've been strung along by the traditional financial institutions that use strict and redundant regulations on how we access our money. Without a good financial background, healthy credit score, or a valuable property to use as collateral, securing a loan with a financial service provider would be a dream for many, and yet that service would be given on a platter for another person in the same queue as you. Why such discrimination? There's no avoiding that with any entity that is run by humans.

This continues to widen the gap between the rich and the poor, simply because some have more access to services that others can only aspire to get. Investment opportunities are only accessed by the privileged while the rest of humankind survives on leftovers. In the process, these financial giants get the lion's share through extortious fees while also bullying the very same clientele that bring them money. This is the problem with centrally run entities. The institutions make more money and give the owners of the funds peanuts after they have serviced themselves with better packages.

Luckily, blockchain technology came to the rescue to remove the intermediaries so that people can serve themselves through a peer-to-peer system that is run by a code. That means the power to do as one pleases with their money is restored into the hands of those who own it. Prior to centralization, people were able to serve one another through bartering. Although it had its limitations, hence smart bankers stepped in, people were able to get services from amongst themselves with no stringent measures and regulations put in place by centralized entities.

Decentralized finance (DeFi), through the incorporation of smart contracts, automated market makers (AMMs), and distributed ledger technology, has not only restored community-based financial models, but has also provided an immutable, transparent, trustless, and permissionless financial system that best serves users regardless of their background. Without a need for tedious paperwork, redundant policies, and threats of censorship, DeFi platforms are growing exponentially amongst the early adopters.

This book was thus written to bridge the gap between the ones who are already benefiting from this wonderful system and the late adopter who is grappling at straws looking for a safe learning environment to learn at their pace the ins and outs of this gigantic concept.

You will soon realize how easy it is to access financial services from a wide range of platforms through a guided manual on which ones offer palatable returns, a great user interface (UI), variety of high yielding instruments, security, and overall best user experience. You will learn how to earn passive income through lending, borrowing, yield farming, and becoming a liquidity provider, to see first-hand the potential of DeFi as well as how it is going mainstream as it gets incorporated in several other sectors.

With *Mastering Decentralized Finance (DeFi)*, your basic knowledge of blockchain technology will expand as we look into market analysis and trading strategies, decentralized insurance, and derivatives while growing a diversified portfolio. The topic on risks involved and challenges will teach you how you can manage funds securely and avoid unnecessary losses. You will also keep up with the trending industry narratives and how you can take advantage of early access to non-fungible tokens (NFTs), the long-awaited metaverse, and how to position yourself better for Web 3.0 adoption. Whichever chapter you want to start with, I welcome you to travel with me through the depths of the pages of this informative and thrilling write-up.

Chapter 1: Understanding the Basics of DeFi & WEB 3.0

Web 3.0 Changing the Global Arena

What the Heck is Web 3.0?

Almost every day when you scroll on the news channels, social, and financial platforms, the term that is trending is Web 3.0. It has surpassed the magnitude at which the Fourth Industrial Revolution (4IR) was on people's tongues several years ago. You may know that there is Web 2.0 and Web 1.0, but do you know exactly what these concepts mean? If you already know this information, kudos to you, you may proceed to the subsequent chapters that are more in depth with DeFi. But for now, allow me to bring light to someone who needs to understand the foundation of the internet, the current state we are in, and the fascinating future of Web 3.0.

Let me make a few assumptions to find a common ground with you. If you are reading this book, I have no doubt that you are a web user, that you surf the internet for information, and that you at least have one social platform. Your interest in DeFi tells me that you already know that we are currently in the social web or Web 2.0. However, allow me to recap and take a short trip down memory lane of the computer class by reminding you that the world wide web was founded in 1990 by *Sir Tim Berners-Lee* after he had realized the difficulty of accessing and sharing information. It was in 1989 at CERN when Berners-Lee, a British computer scientist, proposed this invention to his then boss, *Mike Sendall*, who noted that the proposal was vague but exciting (World Wide Web Foundation, 2018). After Sendall gave Berners-Lee time to work on his proposal, this pioneer of the web successfully wrote three fundamental technologies that make up the web today:

- HTML—Hypertext Markup Language is the formatting language for the web.
- URI—Uniform Resource Identifier, and its commonly known variant, the Uniform Resource Locator (URL), is a unique address (link) used to identify the resource on the web.
- HTTP—Hypertext Transfer Protocol allows retrieval of linked resources across the web.

Berners-Lee designed the web in such a way that there is no central authority. He vouched for decentralization in order to allow the web community to post anything on it as long as it was non-discriminatory, universal—all computers must speak the same language to each other irrespective of location or culture of users—and developed in full view of anyone who wanted to participate on the web. This was made possible by putting a consensus in place. Thus, an internet for all was invented. Because of few contributors in the beginning, Web 1.0 is therefore described as a content delivery network (CDN) consisting of static pages whereby there were more consumers of delivered data than content creators (Sharma, 2018). It was also known as read-only because users could not login, comment, or view analytics; instead, they could only consume what was given.

As time went on and technology advanced, the need to have a more interactive world wide web arose where users would be able to generate content and socially participate on platforms that permit accessing, sorting, and commenting on given information, as opposed to Web 1.0 where content was one-way. In 2001, when the dot-com bubble burst and many concluded that the web was overhyped, others saw this as a turning point, not a crash. This led to a brainstorming session between O'Reilly Media and MediaLive about Web 2.0 (O'Reilly, 2005).

Web 2.0 allows an interactive, accessible, and retrieval of information among site owners and site users by means of evaluation and online commenting (Sharma, 2018). With Web 2.0, the end-users don't just consume delivered content on the site but they can participate too, making it more social than its predecessor. Currently, we're in the Web 2.0 era with access to tools like our social network tags, podcasts, blog posts, and the ability to advocate for or vote against delivery of web content. Websites don't just feed us content, but we can input our data onto the web so that it customizes the kind of content we want to see. It's two-way data traffic where both the site and the user can share opinions.

One of the challenges faced by today's type of internet is its centralization, which is prone to cyber attacks, server malfunctions, and harboring of information from an individual or single authority (Rees, 2022). This means that a website can be killed without you as the user being notified as we have seen with most scam websites that are deleted after they've served their purpose; all you see is *error 404*. Another challenge with Web 2.0 is the lack of privacy for user data as the websites where we input our data sell it to advertisers (Whiteboard Crypto, 2021).

Third parties are able to contact us or pop-up on our screens based on our search history and data that the websites we spend time on collect about us.

Ever noticed how most websites ask you to sign in with Facebook or your Google account? Or how about getting the same YouTube ad based on your latest search topic? Let me make a practical example: I recently visited a virtual private network (VPN) site to upgrade my subscription which I abandoned midway to do it later, and since then every ad that pops up on my YouTube profile or any webpage I'm browsing is of… you guessed it, that exact VPN site.

As with the core of the book, decentralization of the internet is a fancy concept that we look forward to, based on what we're about to learn about blockchain technology and the future it promises. A new concept, Web 3.0, thus circulates amongst us in an intriguing manner that leaves us curious on what exactly it is. Based on what we know about decentralization, by stripping away power from a central authority, Web 3.0 promises openly distributed data that no single entity can tamper with undetected.

As Berners-Lee envisioned back in 1999, Web 3.0 would be what is known as the Semantic Web, which would incorporate use of artificial intelligence (AI) to solve problems like unclear search series and the use of linguistic context (CoinMarketCap, 2021). This means that Web 3.0 will be anchored by automation through the assistance of AI and decentralized autonomous organizations (DAOs), which will be elaborated further in the next chapter.

Incorporating AI features with decentralization results in more user control. This concept, imagined by one of the early developers of Web 1.0 and Web 2.0, *Jeffrey Zeldman* over 16 years ago, is the next evolution of the internet that advocates for the secure sharing of the world's information using the blockchain technology (Rees, 2022). Web 3.0 suggests that you are not just an interactive consumer of content, but you own the content you share. Just like when the sites we visit capture and share our data for profit, third parties will pay you instead, and most likely in crypto.

As we deeply dive into blockchain next, it's imperative to note that decentralization is the core of Web 3.o, and understanding DeFi protocols is what will give us a clear idea of the next phase of the internet, interoperability and the metaverse; thus, changing the world of the web as we know it.

Basics of Blockchain and Decentralized Finance

Basics of Blockchain and Distributed Ledger Technology

We can say the web era opened further channels for technologists to invent solutions and ways of conduct for efficiency and effectiveness in businesses or other sectors. How humans access information on the internet poses a threat of fraudulent activities and misconduct. It's mainly because different sites can display different information and it could go undetected. Unless the need to link that information arises, only then would it be clear that there are falsified elements in shared information. As much as it serves as an expansive source of information, Wikipedia is one of the least credible sources of information due to its ability to be edited by anyone; which means some data shared may contain errors. Therefore, it should not be easily accepted without some form of scrutiny or due diligence to get the facts straight. Anyone can add or delete data on Wikipedia without proper screening of the source or doing proper fact-checking.

A clever system called the blockchain was thus invented to ensure that shared data is the same across servers, accurate, and distributed across the public digital ledger. All computers connected to a blockchain network, called nodes, are responsible for receiving data and sorting it out.

Then advanced miners, with further abilities, distribute the data to where it must reach. Miners are nodes that are qualified to go beyond recording and analyzing data; they have authoritative powers to distribute information across the network. Blockchain technology comes to serve as a governing standard to ensure that members of the network comply with regulations.

By use of Distributed Ledger Technology (DLT), users can be sure of the following aspects with regard to the data transferred. First, it is unanimous—even if the servers are apart, the information that is shared on the blockchain has to be agreed upon by all members (nodes / connected computers) of the network that have the same information as proof of authenticity. Second, it is immutable—all transactions recorded on the blockchain cannot be tampered with, deleted, reversed, or edited, ensuring that the information that is recorded tallies with the one on the brief or as programmed.

With regards to decentralized finance, blockchain technology is the core architecture that anchors the intended functions of DeFi. Without a blockchain, DeFi would not be what it is today. It would be no different from traditional financial platforms that are governed by a central authority. But with DeFi, there is no one who has all the authority to make financial decisions such as determining who is qualified to lend or borrow money. All involved parties can propose conduct and unanimously reach consensus of how a financial system should operate.

In a central and traditional financial system, there is a higher authority that can overrule other members and come up with decisions. Even regulations or standards of operation can be changed by a single authority, affecting users. Blockchain prohibits this through automated agreements that are self-executional, and the distributed public ledger which is open and accessible to everyone in the network, whose steps are traceable to the last command.

The History of Blockchain

Although the blockchain technology is accredited to the mysterious founder or founders of Bitcoin (the world's first and most famous decentralized digital currency), *Satoshi Nakamoto,* after they published the Bitcoin white paper—an instructional document created to give a clear roadmap of the project's intended vision, how it will operate, and the team behind it—in 2008; the term is fairly old. Blockchain was conceptualized by *Stuart Haber* and *W. Scott Stornetta* in the early '90s. The duo described the term as cryptographically secured chains of blocks (ICAEW, n.d.).

Although Bitcoin is recognized as the first globally accepted crypto, there are several attempts at the decentralization of money that precede it. One of the earliest pioneers is DigiCash by *David Chaum,* which was created in 1982. DigiCash was rolled out as *Blind Signatures for Untraceable Payments* and operated between 1982 and 1998, before it declared bankruptcy (Frankenfield, 2021). Another notable mention of early crypto attempts include Bit Gold, which was created a decade earlier than Bitcoin by a computer scientist, *Nick Szabo,* who is also known as the father of smart contracts—self-executing computer programs written on the blockchain (CoinFox, 2015).

What is DeFi?

DeFi is a concept that was born in 2018 in a Telegram group chat between Ethereum developers and entrepreneurs including *Blake Henderson* of 0x, *Brendan Forster* of Dharma, and *Inje Yeo* of Set Protocols (Russo, 2021). The team was discussing what to call the public financial application built on the Ethereum blockchain. In order to better explain DeFi, we'll compare it to the traditional financial system which is run by a central entity like a bank or a private financial service provider. Banks are the money machines, in charge of how money moves amongst us as individuals, businesses, institutions, and countries. These central authorities govern the way we access, transfer, receive, and invest money as long as it is in their system. Banks are run by humans which pose a threat of human error, fraud, extortions, unfair policies, and regulations, which make it difficult to freely access and use money as we please.

Banks charge users outrageous fees for any transaction made because that is how they make money. The 2008 crisis bailouts exposed the shortfalls of the traditional financial systems and opened room for improvement (Penn, 2019). Let's tackle three of the key segments of the banking system and how DeFi smoothes them.

Transaction Delays and Charges

Although it is your money that you want to pay or send to someone, you are not entirely free to access it as banks need you to comply with certain regulations such as the anti-money laundering policies, which will involve you providing extensive documentation to verify where you are sending funds to, and their intended purpose. Sure, it is ethical to comply with these policies, but the actual service delivery of banks can be a pain that brings delays (hours to several days, and weeks in some cases) through data capturing and verification. On top of that, it's expensive to send money through banks, service fees, cross-border (international wire inbound and outbound) charges, and foreign exchange fees.

With DeFi however, which is powered by cryptocurrencies, sending funds across the globe is a matter of seconds to a couple of minutes with a huge cut down on fees. You can literally send crypto to someone in another continent while you're still on call with them and they can immediately verify that they have received the funds. These funds can be accessed right away, instead of waiting for them to be cleared as with the banks. Clearance includes putting the source of funds and reason for sending them under scrutiny.

DeFi gives you control over your money, the freedom to use it any way you want, which central authorities are against. They are constantly looking for ways to restrict us from doing as we please with our hard-earned money. There is no waiting period or delays for funds to be cleared. Because of self-executing transactions programmed in DeFi protocols, like when to release funds during lending, checking collateral for borrowers, or calculating interest due to liquidity providers, there is no staff dedicated to do these tasks as with the bank, cutting fees tremendously.

Centralization and Transparency

Traditional systems are governed by a single body with authority to make changes, enforce policies, and change regulations. This authoritative body is made up of humans, which can fail in governance, due to corruption, miscalculation, or any human error. One wrong decision on policies enforced by those in power can cause the whole financial model to crumble. The 2008 crisis where over 500 banks in the US failed and billions of dollars were lost is proof of this. That is because a lot of governance happens at the backend where the public cannot see red flags looming to a failure.

This is not the case with DeFi platforms as everything is openly recorded on the public digital ledger. No single person can sway the direction of the way a DeFi platform should operate. In fact, anyone who attempts to tamper with the programmed code is not only detected, but they are kicked out of the network. Moreover, smart contracts are programmed to verify and approve transactions only when set parameters are met, so there is no cheating the system. With the bank, an authority can secretly remove or edit a transaction to suit their needs, while this can never happen on decentralized networks because any suggested edit is cast out to the network where it is validated. If it can't be verified, it is rejected.

Accessibility and Censorship

Not everyone has access to financial assistance in central institutions due to some restrictive policies, particularly in developing countries. A taint to your reputation may be the reason you are not getting a fair service from the bank. The bank may decide that due to your previous misconduct, you should be denied a loan or access to a certain bank account type. There are plenty of discriminative factors that make getting access to fair financial services difficult. The same thing applies in the case where you are suspected of misconduct or someone has falsely put a claim on your behavior, banks can freeze or close your accounts until your name is cleared. This means that you don't really have complete access to your accounts as you please, you cannot even travel internationally without alerting your bank that you will need to access your accounts from a foreign country.

With DeFi, you are just a nameless profile; what you do in your personal capacity does not have a bad effect on your crypto accounts. DeFi protocols are run by a written code that does not discriminate or know anyone personally. We are all equal on DeFi platforms. No one is more influential than the other, nor can anyone sway conduct to suit their own needs. Even in countries where people don't have access to equal financial treatment, DeFi squashes that. You can access your funds anytime and anywhere without restrictions. You can qualify to take out loans as you please in censorship-free decentralized platforms.

Characteristics of DeFi

Borderless

Anyone with an internet-connected smartphone can have access to DeFi protocols regardless of where they are in the world. Sending remittances across the globe has been made super easy because cryptocurrencies know no geographical jurisdictions. There are no international wire inbound and outbound fees, or any foreign exchanges fees. Someone in Africa can access a loan from any DeFi platform, without the need to provide any form of documentation or personal details that can be restricted in their specific country. In turn, someone in China can invest in DeFi by lending their money on the DeFi platform and make great returns, something that would not be accessible from their country that banned crypto miners (Che, 2021). With DeFi, there are no barriers that can restrict how and where money is sent or accessed from.

Trustless

There is no need to trust anyone as is the case with financial institutions. You need to be able to trust the centralized authorities that are in charge of your money and because they are run by humans, they are bound to make mistakes or intentionally defraud the system; thus, your funds are not entirely safe. With DeFi, there is no institution in charge of your funds. You are your own bank, with all the private keys in your control. There is no human error because of the incorporation of smart contracts which will only execute according to the written code.

Fast

Besides lengthy periods of sending money across the globe, having instant access to your funds is questionable with financial institutions. Banks usually invest your money and profit from it, hence you would need to notify them before you access it (if you have a fixed investment, of course). The period that can be long and defeat the purpose in the case of an emergency. With DeFi, you have instant access to your funds. Efficiency is key with DeFi.

Composable

The composability of DeFi is the reason that it is considered to be money Legos due to its ability for other apps and functions to be built on its protocols or decentralized applications (DApps) that can be accessed from different sites, making interoperability an ease (Boyan, 2020). For instance, you can take out a Dai loan on Compound, split it and put half on Oasis, and the other half on another protocol with a leveraged position to make more interest. Then you can use the interest to settle your loan and still have extra funds in Compound; all using one smart contract. That's how composable and programmable DeFi is.

Non-Custodial

You are in charge of your private keys and passwords. Centralized institutions usually keep your keys so that they can help you restore them in the event that you lose them. But as long as you don't have full control of your money, you're still at risk of embezzlement, hacking, or any form of bank run. With most DeFi protocols, your funds remain in non-custodial wallets. This means that you're the only one responsible for the safekeeping of your funds. Some protocols even allow you to loan or provide collateral with your funds without sending them from your cold wallet for extra security.

Transparent

Everything is openly done on the blockchain, making it easy for contributors to suggest improvements of service and for smart contracts to be audited. You don't know everything that the bank does with your money while it's in their custody. Whatever gambles they take, you only know when something is wrong, when the bank needs a bailout or declares insolvency that they dabbled with your funds and made their own profits in the process. DeFi protocols are transparent. Whatever happens to the liquidity provided is openly recorded on the public ledger. There are no surprises with DeFi.

Busting the Decentralization Myths

Part of the reason why some people are slow to adapt to decentralization is that there is a lot of misinformation going on in this space. It's granted that it's not an easy concept to comprehend at first. In this section, we'll bust the common myths about decentralization and correct this misconception.

DeFi Will Never Go Mainstream

It depends on whether this means that DeFi will never overtake traditional finance or whether it will not be globally accepted and adopted for every financial service offered by centralized finance. The former may be true, considering that traditional finance amasses quadrillions of market cap, compared to DeFi that is just below $100 billion, or the crypto market as a whole which is just below two trillion dollars (CoinGecko, 2022b).

Traditional finance has been there for the longest time, and that gives it an advantage over a less than five-year-old DeFi, and just over a decade-old crypto market. At the rate of its adoption, DeFi is disrupting traditional finance, and its deployment in many financial services like lending, borrowing, asset management, and insurance, is gradually gaining traction, and given enough time, DeFi has a great potential to go mainstream. If it wasn't already disrupting traditional finance, it wouldn't be facing so much criticism and slaps of regulation hints by central authorities.

DeFi is Complicated

While this is true to some extent, it is not entirely the case. Every new technology is disruptive and complex at first, but we cannot become experts at it unless we give it a go. It's amazing how the masses who labeled blockchain technology as one complex entity are actively seeking a basic understanding of the industry. Check the Google stats for NFT searches in the past year, and the results of that search, together with the metaverse and Web 3.0 will blow your mind! It's only once the people are won over to the crypto side that they understand that DeFi is not that much complex, neither is the underlying technology.

People will always make time to learn something that they are interested in. As DeFi is still starting out, soon it will not be put in the same sentence with complexity. Decentralization will be a huge part of our lives, and people will wonder how at one point they thought it's too difficult to understand. Just as the internet was clunky to use in its early days, especially prior to the world wide web, transformation just needs a few tweaks to the interface and it starts to work like second nature (Duke University, n.d.).

DeFi is Mainly Used for Illegal Activities

Arguably, crypto is used for illegal activities to some extent, but to say mainly is a little exaggeration. The dark web marketplace, Silk Road, is probably one of the largest contributors to making Bitcoin a notorious currency for illegal activities. Silk Road was censored by the FBI in 2014, less than five years into the decentralized world (60 Minutes Australia, 2014). We cannot still believe that almost 15 years later, the main reason people use cryptocurrencies is for malicious behavior. That would mean that we're oblivious to all the innovations, the implemented use cases mentioned in this book, as most of them are what we see giving this industry credit. So, yes, the early adopters of decentralization were thugs and bad actors, but DeFi is now used for good services. If countries are adopting decentralization, that must count for something. Cash is still the main thing used for rendering and paying for illegal services as it's not traceable, unlike most cryptocurrencies today. It is said that 79% of the US currency is in $100 bills, and is regarded as prone to malicious use (Duke University, n.d.).

Government CBDC Will Put Crypto Out of Business

While it's true that a large number of people who have not yet or are late to adopt crypto still trust banks and are more likely to trust bank-issued stable coins or central bank digital currencies (CBDC), there is a huge difference between these and crypto. The main reason people choose crypto is to eliminate intermediaries, red tape, and the constant need to receive permission to transact or explore financial activities. But using CBDCs is like adding a tracker to your crypto activities, so what's the point? And not forgetting that you'll be liable to comply with anti-money laundering (AML) and know your customer (KYC) regulations, enforced to pay taxes, and even censored should you deviate from these rules. Using CBDCs defeats the purpose of blockchain as a whole. While this may work in countries like China, where citizens don't have a choice but to go with what the government imposes after crypto bans, thinking that this will put decentralized finance out of business is wishful thinking (Duke University, n.d.).

Blockchains and DeFi Protocols Are Not Secure and Prone to Hacking

This is actually true. Some blockchains and protocols are vulnerable to malicious behavior. But as you will see throughout this book, there are so many alternatives and ways to avoid being hacked or how to generally stay safe in this industry. But malicious behavior is everywhere, else we wouldn't hear of so much theft, embezzlement, hacking, and heists in the central world (Newman, 2021). With implementations like Web 3.0 wallets, that let the user have full custody of their funds, cold storage, DeFi insurance, and innovative ways to stay safe in this industry, most protocols are making the cost of corruption to be higher than profit from corruption so that people are encouraged to use the blockchain for the right purpose. Of course, we cannot seize all the fraudsters, but the security in decentralized finance is increasingly improving.

DeFi is Over-Hyped but With No Future

This statement is common also with respect to NFTs or the blockchain industry when it started. It's easy to assume that a certain technology is just a passing phase, and then it turns out to be one of the biggest innovations around how everything is centered. Remember when the dot-com bubble burst and that was the pivotal point for internet-based companies (Hayes, 2019)? That's pretty much what people thought when crypto hits a bear season, amateurs panic selling, and people supposedly quitting crypto only to regret it when bull run sets in. With great fundamentals surrounding most DeFi protocols, and services at large, DeFi is worth the hype. All that you need is to ladder your purchases and know when to enter and exit the market. Do your own research and this hype will be one of the most valuable things you encounter.

Key Terminologies for Web 3.0 and DeFi

It's hard to mention Web 3.0 without the word 'decentralized'. That is why DeFi will play a big role in the integration and on-boarding process of Web 3.0. Both concepts advocate for freedom, and control in ownership; like Web 3.0 wallets being used in DeFi, giving full custody to users, and the fact that Web 3.0 in its sense will be integrated on the blockchain in a decentralized manner. Below are some of the key features that overlap between Web 3.0 and DeFi.

Openness

The key features of any of these two concepts include using an open-source code that is accessible to the community of users and developers in full view of the public.

Trustless

There is no need to trust any intermediary that it will not expose your data to third parties. You fully own your content and you can share it as it pleases you, without fear that it will be accessed without your permission or that your trust will be broken.

Permissionless

There is no need to ask permission to join or access either concept. Both are permissionless, hence there's freedom to enter, exit, access and retrieve data without having to comply with a central authority that can impose laws that put you in a box.

Edge Computing

Edge computing refers to processing data at the edge or the periphery of the network that ensures that data has more places to travel to by shortening the distance it has to travel. It improves time to action, reduces response time to milliseconds, conserves network resources, allows 5G connectivity, and ensures that data is as close to the original source as possible (Bigelow, 2021). The shift to Web 3.0 means moving data from the center to the edge, and sometimes directly to the hands of the user.

Decentralization

A decentralized data network enables content creators to sell or trade their data without the risk of losing rights to ownership, risking their privacy, or depending on intermediaries. This means that users will own their content instead of in Web 2.0 where third parties are given access to your information for a fee that you don't receive, and your history is recorded and tracked without your consent. Pretty much, that's how you're able to get a loan on DeFi where it's just you interacting with a smart contract and no central authority that tracks your activity and even sells your data to third parties.

Artificial Intelligence and Machine Learning

Artificial intelligence (AI) and machine learning (ML) algorithms when built on decentralized networks advance to make valuable, precise, and life-saving acts. That explains why they go beyond targeted precision materials, medication creation, and climate modeling without the human error factor. Embedding AI and ML to Web 3.0 will allow platforms to distinguish genuine data from fraudulent and rigged information (Bhattacharya, 2021).

Blockchain

As already mentioned, blockchain technology is the backbone of Web 3.0. Without it, Web 3.0 would have no foundation. Just like DeFi protocols that run on the Ethereum blockchain through smart contracts, Web 3.0 aims at enhancing data privacy and control, great front-end, seamless services, transparency, and open accessibility to data on permissionless platforms (Bhattacharya, 2021).

Chapter 2: Mastering Blockchain and DeFi

Blockchain Networks and Composition

In order to master blockchain and decentralized finance, you need to understand the core of this technology. This chapter will breakdown how blockchains are composed, different elements that constitute as building materials of this structure, standards involved, consensus mechanisms, and the different networks available. It's from the basic terms that this rather complex technology has been simplified through examples.

Types of Blockchain Networks

There are numerous blockchains in existence today, to sum them up, they are categorized into four main networks.

Public

As the name suggests, public blockchain can be accessed by anyone because data is distributed on a public ledger. There is no permission needed for anyone to transact or participate on this type of network. Public blockchain is the first known blockchain network, and it is well depicted by the iconic work of Satoshi Nakamoto on Bitcoin. Other blockchains that use this network include Ethereum, Litecoin, and NEO. Because information is openly accessible to anyone, this type of blockchain is completely decentralized, and cannot be manipulated. However, there is a need for governance for an orderly function of every blockchain.

In order to accurately validate transactions on this trustless peer-to-peer network, a consensus has to be reached. Therefore, there are nodes and miners that participate in the validation process and are kept motivated by rewards in the form of cryptocurrencies. Anyone within this distributed network, in possession of good mining power, can participate in the validation process and receive mining rewards. Public blockchain uses consensus mechanisms such as proof-of-work (PoW) and proof-of-stake (PoS) protocols. Below are some of the notable advantages of using this type of blockchain network:

- Public blockchains are non-restrictive, giving complete access and freedom to users.
- Users' identity is protected because of this blockchain's anonymity.
- There is no need for anyone to trust another; the system itself is trustless and completely transparent as transactions are publicly recorded on the open and distributed ledger.
- The fact that this blockchain is not run by a central authority makes it trustworthy, especially knowing that no one has that much control to kill the project. Even though we don't know the real identity of Satoshi Nakamoto, or anyone else who contributed to the success of Bitcoin, the blockchain will exist eternally. The same applies for the Ethereum blockchain. Even if Vitalik Buterin decides to leave the project, as did the seven co-founders, Ethereum blockchain will continue to function.

A public blockchain network does, however, face a number of shortcomings that make it a bit undesirable for certain functions. Below are some of the cons:

- This is the most congested blockchain, making transactions utterly slow to validate. This also makes it hard to scale.
- The fact that it is open to everyone does not exempt attackers from gaining access. If hackers can control 51% of the network,

they can disrupt it and people's funds will be compromised in the process.

Private

Without a question, a private blockchain entails a hidden network as data is only accessible to those who are invited to join the network. It is not open to the public outside of a private organization, hence it is also called permissioned or closed network. Usually, this network has a central authority seeing to it that the blockchain functions as intended. Private blockchains give organizations access to record data on the blockchain while maintaining their privacy from their competitors. Private blockchains are mainly used in the supply chain, internal voting, and asset ownership entities. Some of the pros of private blockchain are listed below:

- Private blockchains are fairly safer than public blockchains because only invited participants have access to the network, mitigating the risk of having attackers invade the network.
- They are also super fast compared to other blockchains, as they are only open to a smaller network. This means that they also scale more as it takes less time to validate and reach finality of transactions.
- Organizations using this network have complete control over which miners can validate transactions and create new blocks, and which nodes can view which part of the data and make changes.

Below are some of the cons of a permissioned network:

- The main shortcoming of a private blockchain is that it's vulnerable because it can have a single point of failure. The central authority can pull the plug at any time, making it not so secure outside of the scope of its intended use.

- Data can be manipulated on private blockchains, even if they claim to be audited; chances of foul play are there.
- There are controversies that, because they don't conform to the core principles of blockchain, decentralization, private blockchains are not true blockchains (Parizo, 2021).

Hybrid

Hybrid blockchains merge both the elements of public and private blockchains, offering some organizations the best of both worlds. Organizations have the freedom to choose which data is made public and which is kept confidential. Hybrid blockchains can be used in several organizations that want to partially participate in the decentralized network, to make certain information distributed.

For instance, if it's used by a real estate agency, the entire agency can be run off-chain or on a private network, but certain information like listings and previous sales can be publicly accessed by anyone. By embedding smart contracts, this network can also be used in the medical industry, whereby patients' records can be accessed and used for further research by doctors without the fear of breaching doctor-patient confidentiality as their private data will not be accessed by third parties (Chen et al., 2019).

Here are some of the features that make this blockchain desirable:

- Like private blockchains, the fact that hybrid blockchains operate in a closed network makes it secure and 51% attack-proof, as members of the network are known.
- Because it's a smaller network, there is no congestion in this blockchain, ensuring that transactions are processed and validated at bolt speed. This also means that scalability is higher in this blockchain.

The cons include the following:

- There are no incentives for participants of this network, making upgradability an issue as there are no motivated validators. This means that users do not make it a priority to see that it doesn't fail, or to contribute towards its improvement.
- It is prone to manipulation as it is controlled by a central authority. This also means that it is not transparent, therefore users need to trust the organization, which is not always the case that their loyalty will be rewarded.

Federated or Consortium

This type of blockchain resembles a hybrid blockchain in that it merges private blockchains in its governance. But instead of allowing just one private blockchain to be in charge of the entire network, a number of private entities operate in a decentralized manner to share responsibilities that can be publicly accessed by members of the consortium. Federated networks are governed by a consensus mechanism that uses preset nodes. Validator nodes initiate, receive, and validate data, while member nodes can receive or initiate transactions (Iredale, 2020).

It can be used in food tracking processes, research data, and even in the banking systems where different banks can form a consortium and operate in a decentralized but controlled manner. Examples where a federated blockchain is implemented include: Marco Polo, IBM Food Trust, and Energy Web Foundation.

Pros of this blockchain include:

- It cannot be shut down or manipulated by one single authority as power is shared amongst participating private entities in a decentralized network.
- Risks of a 51% attack are kept to a minimum as members within the network are known.
- It is more scalable than a public network, as there is no congestion in the network and through the use of the well-defined consensus mechanisms.
- Organizations using this blockchain have more access control over what is shared in the network, making it more customizable.

The shortcomings include:

- There is a lack of transparency in the federated network.
- It may be subject to regulations and censorship.
- Unlike public blockchains, this network is not anonymous, which may restrict freedom of participants as they know that they are under surveillance.

Blockchain Composition

As previously explained, blockchain is a connected series of blocks that contain information in a manner that proves its provenance and in such a way that it cannot be manipulated. But how does it work? Blockchain can simply be broken down by viewing its components. The block contains three key components, which include the recorded data, a hash, and the hash of the previous block. Depending on the type of blockchain, recorded data can include a transaction entry that states the amount of crypto being sent, the details of the sender, and the recipient's address. A hash is an encrypted algorithm that is used as a unique block identifier or fingerprint, mapping the particular block and its contents. Changing anything on the algorithm of the hash changes the entire hash, making it a completely different one. This makes a hash to also function as proof of authenticity of a block. Another component contained in a block is the hash from the previous block (Simply Explained - Savjee, 2017).

For instance, the first block will show its identifying hash number 12ZT and no hash for the previous block or 0000, as it is the genesis block. The following block will contain its hash Y8G1 and the previous hash 12ZT, the next will also follow suit and depict 6WB3 as its identity and Y8G1, and so will the succeeding blocks. That chain of blocks containing encrypted information on a public ledger is the blockchain. Tampering with any block or the information it contains changes its identity, or hash, making the succeeding blocks to be different as well as they will be containing a previous block hash that has been altered.

To curb block manipulation, the blockchain uses a proving mechanism that causes the creation of the next block to delay in order for the information to be verified. This is called a consensus mechanism, which also means the agreement reached in the network to prove legitimacy of the block. Different blockchains use different consensus mechanisms to secure their own network. The first known or most popular blockchain, the Bitcoin network, uses PoW consensus, which slows down the block creation by 10 minutes to verify the authenticity of the transaction before creating a new block. Other blockchains use different consensus mechanisms, such as PoS, proof-of-authority (PoA), or proof-of-history, as will be discussed further shortly.

The following terminology also adds toward the composition of the blockchain:

Block Height

This refers to the number or position of a block between itself and the genesis block. For instance, the genesis block has the block height of zero, since there is no other block positioned before it (Crypto Corner, 2019). The blockchain explorer shows this information in a programming language, including the block size, timestamp, and other components of that block. If a block's height is 32709128, that means that there are 32,709,127 blocks that come before the particular block, or that is its distance from the genesis block of that blockchain. The block height cannot be used to identify a particular block as different blocks can compete for the same position yet they contain different data.

Block Size

Block size is the capacity of blocks, or the size of files that can be contained in a single block. Bitcoin's block size for the most part of its life span is said to be one megabyte. There are controversies around that, especially after Bitcoin forked to Bitcoin Cash, which has a block size of 32 megabytes (Crypto Corner, 2019).

Block Time

This is the time it takes for a blockchain to generate a new block and is dependent on the difficulty of a particular blockchain, for instance, it takes 10 minutes for a new block to be created in the Bitcoin blockchain. For blockchains like Litecoin, block time is two and a half minutes, and for Ethereum it's 15 seconds.

Throughput on the other hand is a measure of transactions that can be computed by a blockchain in a given period. And it is measured in transactions per seconds, minutes, or hours (TPS, TPM, or TPH). Throughput differs depending on the complexity of transactions. For instance, generally, Ethereum has a high throughput than Bitcoin, but there are times when Bitcoin throughput can be faster than that of Ethereum; when Ethereum is used in complex transactions like minting NFTs, whereas Bitcoin is used simple to transfer assets from one wallet to another (Alexandria, n.d.).

Finality is the time taken to complete a blockchain transaction in such a manner that it guarantees its permanence. Once a transaction has reached its finality, it cannot be reversed or lost (Ifegwu, n.d.). Finality is dependent on the latency of a blockchain, or the time it takes for an input to result in a desired output (time between casting a transaction to a network and its confirmation). As already established, Bitcoin's block time takes 10 minutes, but its finality is about 60 minutes with six confirmations.

Nonce

Short for a number that can only be used once, a nonce is the arbitrary number that miners need to guess. Miners compete by using their computing power or hash rate to be the first one to come up with this number (Kotamraju, 2019). Once a nonce has been found, the new block is added on the blockchain and miners receive mining rewards for solving that algorithm. With Bitcoin blockchain and other blockchains that use PoW consensus mechanism, a nonce is determined by trial and error computational methods, which is why PoW is regarded as bad for the environment due to the energy required to solve this algorithm and the carbon emitted in the process.

Timestamp

Block timestamp is the exact record of when the block was created and a transaction was processed in the blockchain. Every transaction has its own timestamp. Timestamp should not be confused with block time above. For instance, the genesis block of Bitcoin has a timestamp of 2009-01-03 20:15, which can never be erased as this is when the first Bitcoin was mined.

Consensus Mechanisms

Technically speaking, a consensus mechanism is a fault-tolerant protocol used in blockchain networks to reach an agreement of how a particular blockchain functions (Frankenfield, 2021b). Every blockchain can have a different consensus than others that uses a number of methodologies to determine trust and logic in a decentralized network. Consensus protocols are implemented to determine whether the block is valid, when the next block will be generated, and which node qualifies to add a new block through computational mathematics. Below are some of the most common consensus mechanisms, but the list is not limited to the protocols mentioned here.

Proof-of-Work (PoW)

This is the first known and most popular protocol as its implementation is seen in the Bitcoin, Bitcoin Cash, Ethereum, and Litecoin networks. It involves miners competing to do computational work to generate the next block. Miners with a higher hash rate, aim to reach the solution to the algorithm fastest, and therefore show their PoW.

Only once the work done and submitted proves to be satisfactory, can the miner add a transaction and qualify for block rewards.

Due to its difficulty, an attacker would need to control 51% of the network to manipulate the system, which is why it consists of miners who mainly play by the rules and compete fairly to get the mining rewards. As already established, PoW requires a lot of energy, making it more expensive and slow to mine crypto, and validate transactions as opposed to other protocols. However, it is disliked for the carbon footprint it leaves, which is harmful to the planet.

Proof-of-Stake (PoS)

Also known as staking, this consensus mechanism entails users of a blockchain staking their crypto or locking it away from their immediate access wallets so that it is used to validate transactions in the blockchain. The more locked crypto, the better the chances of being chosen to create the next block. Unlike mining where users compete to become validators, here validators are randomly picked based on the amount of crypto staked. Instead of mining rewards, users get staking rewards.

Because there is no need for computers (nodes) or servers (rigs) that use a lot of energy, PoS is an efficient alternative that also brings scaling solutions to the network. It is environmentally friendly. Projects that use this consensus mechanism include: Avalanche, Cardano, Solana, and the anticipated Ethereum 2.0.

Delegate Proof-of-Stake (DPos)

Similar to PoS, DPos consensus requires users to stake their crypto. The only difference here is that users with more coins staked get to vote to elect validators of the block, hoping that they will represent them well in the network, and possibly share some of their staking rewards with them. The problem with this methodology is that whales can influence the votes by electing their friends or themselves in order to control the network, this poses a threat of 51% attack. Blockchains that use DPos include Klaytn, BitShare, and EOS networks.

Proof-of-Authority (PoA)

Founded by Ethereum co-founder and former CTO, *Gavin Wood* in 2017, PoA is another viable alternative consensus algorithm that uses authorities instead of a number of assets staked, or more computational power for a user to qualify as a validator. Users basically need to reveal their identity in order to have authority to become validators of a network (Comben, 2019). In this consensus mechanism, reputation carries more authority than possession of digital assets and computing power.

The PoA protocol has a set of benefits such as being tolerant to 51% attack as validators are people with provable identities, making the protocol one of the most secure algorithms. Also, because there is no need for any expensive hardware, this algorithm is more efficient, and environmentally friendly. The rate at which transactions are validated is also improved as validating authorities are already known, instead of being voted for or competed against in the above protocols. This mechanism is used in projects such as VeChain's POA network.

Proof-of-Capacity / Space

Similar to PoW but instead of using computational power, the proof-of-space mechanism requires users to allocate free storage space in order to get a chance to validate the network or create the next block. In other words, it allows miners to use the free hard drive space from their devices in order to validate transactions. The larger the hard drive space, the more possible solutions the miner can carry, and the better the chances to win the lottery as more guesses will be stored in that space. Projects that use proof-of-capacity include Burstcoin, Storj, and SpaceMint (Hayes, 2021).

DeFi Fund Management

Investing in decentralized finance can be intimidating for most crypto novices, especially with the expansive content of this niche. Knowing which protocol to pursue, or which DeFi platform to lend, borrow, provide liquidity for, or to yield farm from requires experience and determination. In traditional finance, there's a way in which investors can mitigate their risks through a hedge fund or asset management. There are stringent restrictions for one to manage their funds through hedge funds, where it's a must to have a huge account and experience to qualify, and pretty much, everything meant to exclude someone with low startup capital to meet the threshold.

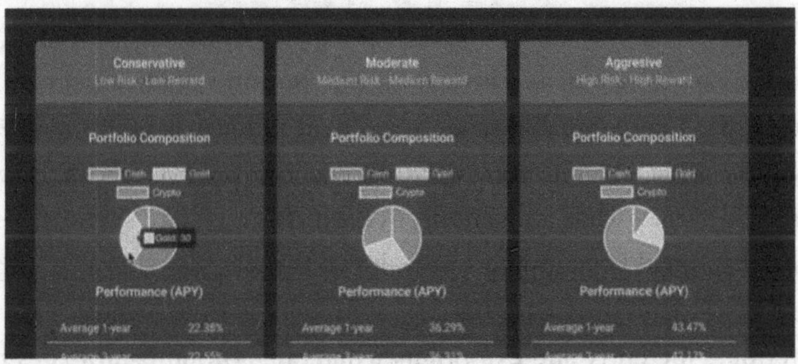

DeFi bridges the gap by allowing beginners to manage their funds irrespective of how much they have on the table, without having to qualify as an accredited investor. The intermediary fund manager in traditional finance is eliminated through DeFi hedge funds, which give full control to users.

With tools like TokenSets, which use algorithms to automatically manage your funds, you can categorize your assets into different sets and aggregate them as you wish, and the algorithm will rebalance your portfolio. If you want a bundle of stablecoins making up a quarter of your entire portfolio, ERC-20 tokens occupying another quarter, and half distributed among yield farms, lending, and trading platforms, the set always remembers and you don't have to manually rebalance your portfolio.

You can choose sets that have a good performance history, but know that historical data doesn't always guarantee that the future will emulate the same results. Based on your research, you can bundle your assets to even out your risk or diversify with different crypto products so that when one sub-niche is performing well, and the others are dragging, you know that the sets will automatically hedge. If you're using the likes of Robo Sets, then it will look for profitable sets and reallocate your assets, rebalance, while actively changing to protocols that offer high APY in order to give optimum results. All this happens without an intermediary as would happen in the traditional fund management.

Robo Sets also have different strategies such as buy and hold, trend trading, range-bound, and inversion. The buy and hold strategy is one of the simplest and arguably safest types as it reduces many movements of jumping from asset to asset. It realigns the portfolio to follow your allocated target while preventing overexposure to any single token and instead of quickly swapping assets, it holds them long-term or until they are in profit. The trend trading approach uses technical analysis to determine the entry and exit points while range-bound automates buying or selling within a predefined range, and inversion is mainly used to trade an assumed benchmark (Belford, 2021, pp. 116–118).

That's the beauty of DeFi, using smart contracts and algorithms to eliminate third parties, save costs, have flexible tools to change your asset allocation as you wish, have time and freedom while your money is making more for you, and you remain in control of your finances. All you need is to do your own research on sets that best suit your needs, or create your own from what your research guides you to. This is further explored in the section on asset management.

Smart Contracts and Crypto Wallets

What Are Smart Contracts?

Coined in 1994 by the renowned computer scientist, *Nick Szabo*, smart contracts are digital, technical agreements that self-execute when predertmined conditions are met. Working on the "if this, then that" logic, Smart contracts are a smart way of reaching consensus on the DeFi protocols, performing tasks without the need of an intermediary to bring order in this trustless system (Whiteboard Crypto, 2021a). Although fairly not a new concept, smart contracts became popular with the launch of Ethereum, Bitcoin's biggest competitor and the second largest world class crypto. Unlike Bitcoin that was mainly designed to facilitate borderless, encrypted, and publicly distributed financial transactions, Ethereum came with a better use case that cemented the lives of developers on the decentralized side. Ethereum is a programmable blockchain, which means that it allows the building of other applications and blockchains on top of it. DApps and smart contracts are the core functions of the Ethereum blockchain.

How do Smart Contracts Function?

In order to understand how a smart contract works, we'll study the following case studies:

Scenario A

Alice wants to buy a house from Bob for 500 ETH ($1,350,000.00), so they both use a smart contract that stipulates that when Alice transfers 500 ETH to Bob, the title deed takes Alice's name, and thus the house is now owned by Alice. *If* the condition of 500 ETH is met, *then* the change of ownership is automatically executed.

What the smart contract eliminated is the need to use a bank, real estate agent, and a lawyer. Cutting these intermediaries has not only cut the fees of this transaction that would have been an addition to the house sale amount, but has also saved the time that the documents would need to go back and forth through the lawyer, the agent, the bank, and between Alice and Bob.

Scenario B

Farmer Joe has taken out insurance for his crops from a decentralized insurance platform; let's call it Save The Farmer. He pays 0.1 ETH monthly to cover him from crop loss. The condition is, if the temperatures exceed 95°C for four consecutive days, then Save The Farmer must pay Farmer Joe 100 ETH to cover his loss of crops. Now, with the help of an oracle, which is a third-party computer program designed to track live feeds in the real world, or in this case, the live temperatures of where Joe's farm is located, the smart contract will use the information to automatically pay Farmer Joe 100 ETH.

Now, this is effortless, efficient, and effective work done by a smart contract. Saving time that would be needed for Farmer Joe to claim his cover from an insurance company, that would need rechecking the system that he's been faithfully paying his premiums. He would also need to provide proof of scorched crops before he receives his insurance payout. But a smart contract uses its "if, then" logic and within seconds, the settlement is done. No middleman, I mean, an oracle is pretty much another type of a smart contract (Kosinski, n.d.).

Benefits of Smart Contracts

Cost Saving

Through elimination of intermediaries, smart contracts relatively reduce the costs of carrying any task that would otherwise be costly. Agents who assume the role of a middleman usually charge a service fee, but smart contracts are just computer programs following a written code; once conducted, they don't need to be paid.

Speed

Also in relation to the elimination of an intermediary, agreements don't have to go back and forth through third parties, and this saves time. Smart contracts are the only thing between users of a protocol and a service being conducted. This direct contact ensures that conditions of an agreement are seen in real time by participating parties, and thus transactions are instantly executed as they're programmed in a speedy manner.

Backup

In a centralized system, there are usually not many copies of files, other than originals shared on the server. In the event of server malfunction, failure, or hacking, data is often lost. This is not the case with decentralization or using smart contracts. Information is publicly distributed across multiple servers or nodes in this case, where it is permanently recorded on the blockchain. In the event of loss of one copy, it can be retrieved from the blockchain. Thus, smart contracts are a great way to backup important information, knowing that it lives forever on the blockchain.

Safety

Except for the intended open source code, data on the smart contract is often encrypted and only accessible to authorized parties, and therefore protected against infiltration.

Accuracy

Because smart contracts follow the embedded code to the last detail, they are often quite accurate with limited human error. I say limited because, at the end of the day, a human being writes the code; if the code is faulty from inception, then this accuracy is not 100%. But if the code is error free, rest assured that the smart contract will execute it as accurately as possible.

Drawbacks of Smart Contracts

As with any technology, smart contracts have their own limitations that still contribute to their slow adoption by the masses.

Delayed Transactions

Sounds counterintuitive, I know, but this is not some days of delays, but a few hours during block congestion. In a way, this is a blockchain drawback than specifically that of a smart contract. When there's a lot of traffic of transactions that need verification in the blockchain, whatever tasks that the smart contracts are trusted to execute are delayed. To curb this, some blockchains may allow you to power that transaction with more gas fee in order to prioritize it in the queue. And some blockchains are working on scalability to reduce block traffic. Other token standards like the ERC-1155 focus on batch transfers to reduce gas fees and block traffic.

Lack of Flexibility

With traditional contracts, there's often room for negotiation based on terms like "good faith" or "reasonable conduct", with which stringent conditions can be eased for an amicable settlement. Smart contracts don't have this kind of flexibility. Once conditions are preset, they have to be adhered to. Otherwise, a new contract would need to be taken out (new code written with new terms). Smart contracts thus, are not flexible to amendments without the need to enter into a new contract, which may be costly to have a new code written. This is even costlier when there's an error in a code, to redo an error-free smart contract would take the same amount of resources it took to make the first faulty contract, something that can be solved with a single call or meeting between parties in a traditional agreement.

Only Partial Elimination of Third Parties

One would assume that taking a smart contract is as easy as clicking a button on a decentralized platform, but it's more complicated than that. Before agreeing to any terms, some people might still need lawyers to verify that the contract conditions are in their best interests. In the above scenarios, though made easy, a typical farmer might not be able to read the smart contract code, without the help of someone who understands Solidity language, or any legal terms. This means that there are hidden costs incurred by someone who needs interpretation of a contract they're taking (Corporate Finance Institute, n.d.).

Uses of Smart Contracts

Crowdfunding

One of the most popular uses of smart contracts can be seen with crowdfunding agreements. If you want to raise funds to support your project, a smart contract can be taken whereby each of your supporters agree to pop up a certain amount of money in turn for a share percentage of your project. When the fundraising goals are met, the money is transferred from the smart contract escrow account to you, and supporters receive the share that you promised. In the event that your goals are not met, the condition is null, therefore, funds are returned to your supporters.

This is common with initial coin offerings (ICOs), token presales, and NFT whitelists whereby project managers need community support to complete implementation of the project and they incentivise members for their support. Members also are able to trust the code, knowing that their promised share will be allocated when the project launches, or that they will receive their money back when the crowdfunding goals are not met.

Flash Loans

During non-collateralized flash loans on DeFi protocols, users can borrow a huge sum of money (crypto) to seize an arbitrage opportunity or to self-liquidate using a smart contract. Because a smart contract pretty much follows the "if, then" logic, it can self-analyze what you've programmed it to do. For instance, if you use a smart contract to take out a flash loan in order to perform arbitrage, it will analyze first if your trade is possible before it executes. In other words, it will check if you will be able to settle the flash loan at the end of that transaction block, which can take a minute or less. If through its analysis it finds that your trade is impossible, maybe due to the current block traffic, it will reject that execution. If it does execute but fails to repay the loan on time, it automatically reverses all transactions of that arbitrage and refunds the flash loan.

Token Switching

Through decentralized exchanges, smart contracts make it easier for traders to swap one token for another. This is made possible because of liquidity providers, especially on assets that would otherwise take a long time to swap on centralized exchanges. Through AMMs, order books are eliminated and thus, smart contracts help in the trading of tokens by determining the price through supply and demand, with a function that has a constant result ($x*y = k$). The existence of a smart contract ensures that k never changes regardless of what happens to x and y. Therefore the price of a token being swapped will change depending on how much of it is available in the liquidity pool as determined by the AMM using the constant formula above.

Healthcare

Smart contracts are used in healthcare systems to record patient's data, and facilitate its access to researchers without breaching doctor-patient confidentiality. An example of this practice can be seen with EncrypGen, which is an application that allows secure transfer of data with limited access to third parties, giving full control to patients on what can be done with their medical records (Laura, 2021).

Supply Chain

In the supply chain, smart contracts are embedded to track the origin, points of sorting, and delivery status of items. If payment must be released upon receipt of goods, the smart contract is able to track the delivery and record the status of the goods. If there is no human intervention needed, then it initiates payment and sends a report that both the sender and the receiver got served accordingly.

Voting

Democratic governance involves people having the right to vote on who they put on the leadership stand, on the regulations that need to be implemented, and on how organizations must run to best serve the communities. Voters do not need to disclose who they voted for, and for transparent votes, smart contracts can be used to prevent double voting, while protecting the identity and choices of voters.

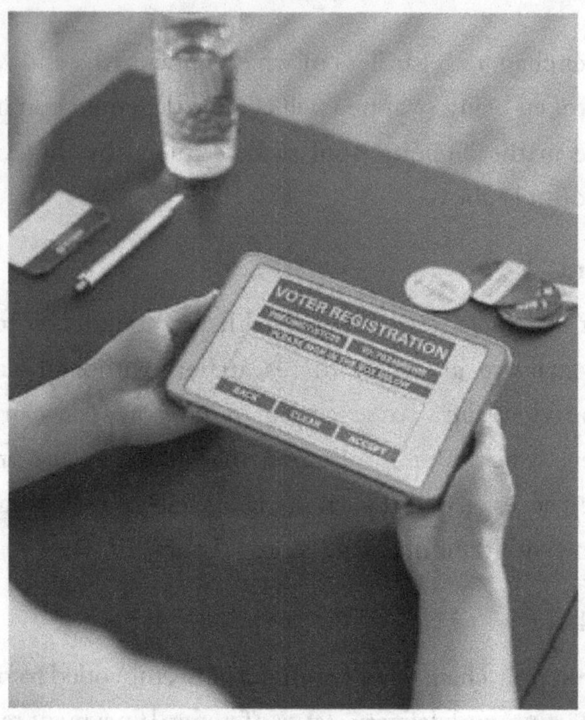

Comparing ICOs and DeFi

What Are ICOs?

ICOs are a form of fundraising done by a team to bootstrap their project by selling a crypto before it officially launches (Daly, 2021). Similar to stock initial public offerings (IPOs), ICOs involve giving a portion of assets to investors in exchange for an equivalent financial contribution. But this contribution does not give the ICO token holders any equity or voting rights as does the IPO. With decentralization, most projects start fundraising for their projects in this way, giving early supporters of a project access to buy their new crypto at a pre-sale price before it launches and get listed on exchanges.

The concept of ICOs was first introduced in 2013 by *J.R. Willet* in the Bitcointalk forum, where he pitched his idea for a protocol to be built on top of the Bitcoin layer to advance the decentralized space with a project that has further utility beyond the payment landscape (Merre, 2021). Willet's proposal was accepted when he successfully launched an ICO of MasterCoin, which raised around $600,000 worth of bitcoin (4,740 BTC, which today is worth around $200 million). Other notable mentions include NextCoin (NEXT), MaidSafe (MAID), and the renowned Ethereum.

Owing to lack of regulation of ICOs, they did not only birth giant, legit projects, they also became a hub for con artists. A lot of rug pulls came along in the form of ICOs and many people lost tons of money in the process. Nonetheless, ICOs still exist, although in decline due to the ban by most countries, including Korea, China, Macedonia, Bolivia, and selected states of the United States (Williams, 2019).

The Rise of IEOs

After the 2017 ICO pump and dump, exchanges also started fundraising to bootstrap their projects in the similar manner and birthed initial exchange offerings (IEOs). A notable IEO happened in 2019 when Binance Launchpad pitched the BitTorrent Token (BTT) in this manner, raising $7.1 million, and sold out within 15 minutes (Bybit Learn, 2021). Because IEOs happen on already established centralized exchanges, investors are more trusting, believing that the exchange's team has done due diligence of the project prior to launching it to their community. A fringe benefit of IEOs is that instead of generating leads to an entirely new bunch of investors, the launchpads occur at exchanges that already have a base clientele, users who don't need to move their funds anywhere but can take action under the same roof, making it easy to participate in.

A comprehensive vetting process that makes IEOs creditworthy over ICOs, along with an already exposed exchange clientbase which prominently reduce marketing fees and listing campaigns for the developers, are some of the contributing factors to the rise of these types of project launches and crowdfunding protocols. However, DeFi on the other hand, does it even better with initial decentralized exchange [DEX] offerings (IDOs). The goal is decentralization, which IEOs have a shortcoming at because they happen on centralized exchanges with the need for KYC approvals and stringent rules. Another drawback is that listing prices for IEOs are hefty for developers, and they don't have full control over their projects as centralized exchanges have more benefits for putting their reputation at stake.

Why IDOs Shine

Initial DEX offerings (IDOs) bring back the power of decentralization to developers and users. Instead of paying ridiculous listing prices on a centralized exchange, developers rely on liquidity providers on DEXs. Another supremacy of IDOs over IEOs is that anyone can participate, unlike with IEOs where users need to move their funds to the specific exchange. Most investors are not comfortable losing custody of their funds, which is the case with custodial centralized exchanges. With IDOs, investors remain custodians of their funds, and thus are even a lesser target to scammers. Since listing tokens on a DEX provides instant liquidity, developers and investors are able to realize profits quicker than with IEOs that involve a future launch date.

However, there are drawbacks in every platform. Both IEOs and IDOs are prone to major sell-offs and pump-and-dump. While prices of ICOs are usually fixed and discounted, giving investors first preference to buy low, participating in IDOs can be quite risky as prices depend on the available liquidity. Buying a token after or alongside a whale, can surge prices while the transaction has already been cast to the network, resulting in fewer coins for the investor at a high price; which is subject to fall a few seconds later when the whales or those who managed to buy first have covered their desired profits.

Chapter 3: Detailed Service Categories and Activities

Exchanges and Stablecoins

DeFi has a number of service categories and activities that highlight its functions. Some of the top categories include exchanges, stablecoins, credit, derivatives, insurance, asset management, lending and borrowing, lottery, and payment services.

Exchanges

As the name suggests, exchanges are marketplaces or platforms where users can swap their fiat for crypto or one digital asset against another. In a central world, these would include foreign currency exchanges where one currency is swapped for another and the exchange house charges a fee. Cryptocurrency exchanges are not only places where different types of digital assets can be bought and sold, but also facilitate global payments and transactions at a minimum fee, allow users to access financial services beyond the traditional finance sector, and are platforms where users can make a living from the comfort of their chosen places of work and devices. These play a huge role in decentralized finance as they are where DeFi services are well executed. The types of exchanges include those run by a central authority and ones run on a peer-to-peer decentralized network.

Centralized Exchanges (CEXs)

CEXs are usually governed by one entity, being a company, organization, or an individual. They offer services like leverage and margin trading where traders can borrow funds from the same exchange in order to increase their trade positions. Central exchanges also provide free custody for users who buy cryptocurrencies in their built-in wallets. They also allow users to make affordable crypto transfers, sending and receiving at a minimal cost.

Most of these exchanges have listed thousands of different cryptocurrencies, including Bitcoin, Ethereum, and numerous other altcoins. Some exchanges like Binance, Coinbase, FTX, Huobi, Gemini, and KuCoin have their native tokens that can be used as the main currency to purchase other listed cryptocurrencies or stake them for rewards. Choosing which exchange to go with depends on several aspects like the trading volume, liquidity, listed assets, the management team, security features, as well as credibility score on ranking platforms such as CoinMarketCap or CoinGecko.

Some instruments may only be accessible through certain exchanges, in which traders can create accounts to access that particular asset and transfer it to a different wallet or use it on decentralized exchanges. Some of the top CEXs are listed below:

Coinbase

Founded in 2011 by *Brian Armstrong*, Coinbase is one of the pioneers of crypto exchanges, making it more trusted and popular amongst global users with over 43 million active users (Vasile, 2021). In 2012, *Fred Ehrsam*, an experienced *Goldman Sachs* trader, joined Coinbase. Coinbase cemented itself high on the crypto exchange ranks in April of 2021, when it went public and listed on Nasdaq (Thorbecke, 2021). Being one of the earliest exchanges, Coinbase has a large number of supported cryptocurrencies.

Not only has it integrated a Web 3.0 wallet, Coinbase Wallet, which is non-custodial, Coinbase is also one of the key players in the NFT space as it partnered with payment behemoth, MasterCard for its upcoming NFT marketplace (Clark, 2022). As mentioned above, Coinbase also has its own native token that is pegged to a US dollar, USD Coin. It is one of the most trusted stablecoins, ranking fifth with a market cap of over $52 billion at the time of writing (Coingecko, 2022).

Binance

Binance is the largest crypto exchange by market cap, credibility score, and the large number of supported cryptocurrencies. Fathered by *ChangPeng Zhao*, who's also known as *CZ*, Binance is a great success for a CEX that was only founded in 2017, and has become one of the most trusted CEXs for a variety of features offered on its platform. Besides being the core endorsement for digital assets listed on this platform, Binance is a home for crypto trading with access to futures, options, margin, and spot trading as well as liquidity pools. Unlike Coinbase above, the UI is a bit complex at face value, but nonetheless, it has great lessons on its website detailing navigating around the platform.

Binance also has a widely traded native coin called the Binance Coin (BNB), as well as a USD-pegged stablecoin, Binance USD (BUSD). Besides having a browser extension wallet, Binance also owns Binance Smart Chain-supported Trust Wallet.

⇆ BTC/BUSD 38942.61 -3.68%

Auto Manual

Recommended parameters are automatically generated based on technical analysis of the symbol price.Details

Lower Price	31443.78 BUSD
Upper Price	46440.66 BUSD
Grid Number	82
Profit/Grid (fees deducted)	0.39% - 0.58%

Copy parameters to Manual settings

Invest Coin BUSD

OKX

Formerly known as OKex, OKX is one of the fast-growing centralized crypto exchanges that gives users a platform to acquire crypto assets, as well as the ability to trade. With low fees on numerous digital assets listed on it, it's no wonder this Seychelles-based exchange that was founded in 2017, continues to rise against all odds. Offering great user experience to the novice and veteran alike, OKX has employed new features that allow users to not only trade crypto assets, but also a lending, staking, and NFT platform (Chan, 2022).

Some of the features include: ability to execute instant trades, a listing of over 250 trading pairs, accessibility on both mobile and desktop, a wide range of deposit and withdrawal methods, P2P trading, secure DeFi Hub, passive income through holding and staking, professional market charts for traders, and an NFT marketplace.

After the platform revamp, OKX also offers a great UI, responsive customer service, as well as useful educational content that novices can benefit from. Holders of OKX's native coin, OKB, have even greater benefits offered on the platform. The only downside about this platform is that of high merchant fees when depositing and withdrawing to third parties. Another drawback is that US residents are not eligible to use the platform.

FTX

The brainchild of the featured Forbes Under 30 and one of the youngest crypto billionaires, *Sam Bankman-Fried* and co-founder *Gary Wang*, FTX is another fast-growing CEX billing itself as an exchange by traders, for traders. One of the newest kids on the block, FTX is a competitive exchange that is increasingly growing its user volume, especially with its lowest rates, a great UI, and its latest NFT marketplace. FTX also has a great portfolio tracking feature that traders love. It has even overtaken the number three spot from KuCoin, cementing its position amongst the top exchanges. FTX also has a separate US version; though it has limited platform features, it has a debit card for US users only (Walters, 2021).

FTX prides itself with relatively low fees, over 300 assets supported, multiple payment and withdrawal options, as well as other earning opportunities like staking rewards with one of the supported coins offering 20% APY! With advanced trading features like trailing stop, limit orders, take profit, and stop loss options, as well as leveraged and futures trading, FTX is designed with a sophisticated trader in mind, while also being beginner-friendly.

KuCoin

Led by CEO and co-founder *Johnny Lyu*, KuCoin is one of the largest CEXs that boasts a large number of users that have been increasing since its launch in 2017. This exchange is known and loved for a number of reasons such as its low fees, bank-level security, and excellent 24/7 customer support (Editorial Team, 2021). Having over 600 cryptocurrencies and over 400 markets, it's no surprise that KuCoin is one of the exchanges prefered by traders, adding to its ability to offer a great trading platform with margin and futures trading features, and low cap coins that have a high potential.

Other upsides for KuCoin include its support to multiple payment options that range from bank wire transfer, debit and credit cards, its support of over 50 fiat currencies, to online payment services like Apple Pay and PayPal. It also offers great discounts to traders who use its native token KCS. KuCoin is a platform that is ideal for both an experienced trader and the beginner alike, with its great UI, multiple earning options like staking and liquidity pools, automated trading, as well as its accessibility on different devices.

While it has been able to be listed among the top exchanges like Binance and Coinbase, KuCoin has received major competition from FTX due to its shortcomings, such as the inability to withdraw fiat and highly competitive rates, which FTX excels at offering lower fees. It however, makes up for these downsides with great support channels and major coin listing (McCracken, 2022).

Decentralized Exchanges (DEXs)

Unlike CEXs, DEXs are not run by a single authority, therefore have no intermediary. However, DEX platforms resemble CEXs in offering trading services, staking, and earning opportunities to users. The difference is that DEXs are governed by smart contracts as written on a code. By using smart contracts, traders can participate in liquidity pools, yield farms, lend and borrow funds, and they can take out insurance without having to trust a service provider. Through automated market makers, there is no need to keep an order book that matches buyers to sellers. Prices are determined by how much of an asset is available in a liquidity pool. DEXs are also non-custodial, which means that users are in total control of their assets and security thereof.

The two types of DEXs are currency-centric and currency-neutral. Currency-centric exchanges depend on the blockchain upon which a DEX is built while currency-neutral exchanges are not dependent on the blockchain and thus, offer a wide range of assets and freedom around the platform. Currency-centric exchanges may restrict or allow assets supported by that particular blockchain. For instance, DEXs built on the Ethereum blockchain support ERC tokens only while those that support currencies from different blockchains are currency-neutral (Johnes, 2019). Below are some of the top DEXs based on their market capitalization rank.

Uniswap

Uniswap is the number one and largest decentralized exchange that uses AMMs that do away with order books but through liquidity pools, and instant peer-to-peer token swaps. It was created in November 2018 by mechanical engineer named *Hayden Adams* with financial injection from a well-known Ethereum developer, *Pascal Van Hecke*, and a series of connections through Adams' friend, *Karl Floersch*. From humble beginnings after losing his job at Siemens, Adams first learned to code on Solidity and was introduced to Ethereum founder *Vitalik Buterin* who asked him to apply for an Ethereum Foundation grant and consider using Vyper to write Uniswap smart contract (Adams, 2019).

Uniswap managed to raise millions of dollars through a series of funding from crypto hedge funds to undisclosed venture capitalists, and collaboration with masters of code to become the number one AMM

DEX that it is today. In January 2021, Uniswap launched its own grant programme to support developers, the same way that its founder received injection to build this protocol. With its UNI token that was also launched in 2020, holders have voting rights on the protocol's governance.

It's worth mentioning that while UNI has performed quite well in 2021 when it reached its all-time high of $44, and currently at less than $9, a large percentage of token holders seem to be whales, which can contribute to spiky movements should any of the whales move their tokens. Nonetheless, Uniswap has over a billion dollars market cap, with 474 supported coins and 938 pairs (CoinGecko, 2022).

Uniswap remains the largest AMM DEX that works well with other DEX protocols like MakerDAO to provide users with access to lending and borrowing protocols. They recently rolled out Uniswap V3 which provides better capital efficiency, accuracy, and prevents short-term loss for liquidity providers. During one of its upgrades, Uniswap forked into another DEX, SushiSwap which takes after it in terms of UI, but generally charges less fees, and has fewer assets.

PancakeSwap

The second largest AMM DEX, PancakeSwap was created by a team of anonymous developers on the Binance Smart Chain in September 2020. PancakeSwap received funding from Binance's $100 Million Fund intended to connect decentralized finance and centralized finance (Coin Bureau, 2021). In terms of coding, PancakeSwap seems to be a clone of UniSwap with enhanced features like built-in yield farms that allow users to stake their liquidity provider (LP) tokens to earn rewards for staking or providing liquidity with CAKE, the native token. Rewards are also in other BEP-20 tokens—Binance Smart Chain token standard that extends Ethereum request for comment (ERC-20). The APYs on these farms and pools is well over 100% and sometimes even over 300% on some farms.

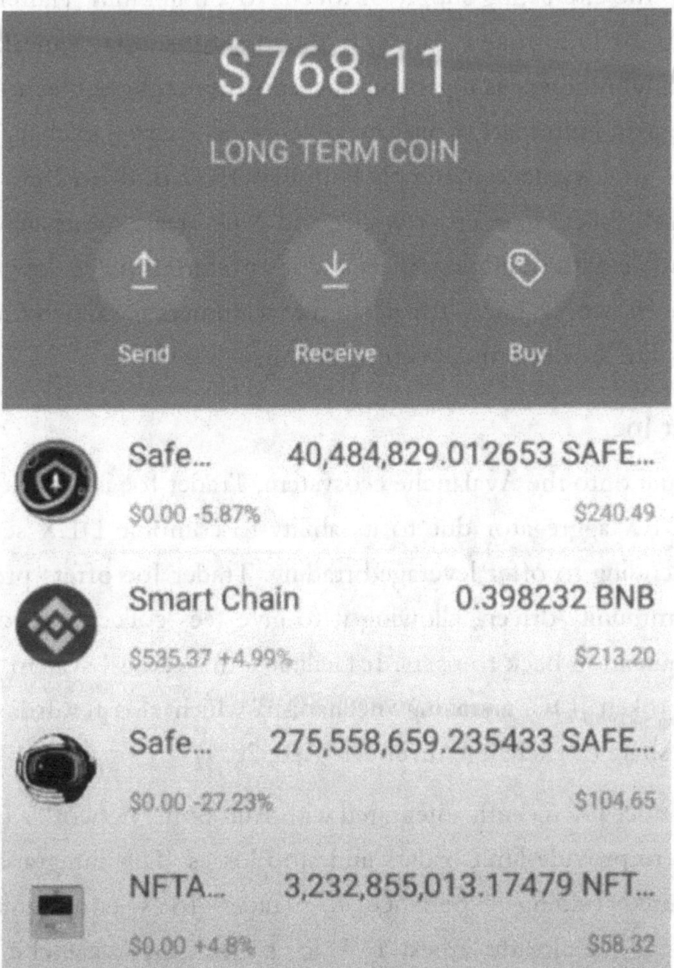

Contrary to its predecessor, PancakeSwap offers relatively low fees to swap tokens, and less block congestion, which is the main reason for Uniswap's atrocious fees. PancakeSwap transactions usually take seconds with the minimal gas fees paid in BNB instead of ETH as is the case with Uniswap. It also grants users quick and easy accessibility to NFTs, initial farm offerings (IFOs), and lottery tickets for a chance of winning big.

PancakeSwap native token CAKE does not have a hard cap, which is a major downside as it means it could be highly inflationary. However, they seem to have deflationary counter-activities like massive token burns to keep the circulating supply of tokens to a minimum (Hamilton, 2021). With its BEP-20 token standard, it's no surprise that PancakeSwap has increasing numbers as it generally accepts more tokens that are not ERC-20 like its counterpart, Uniswap. Binance centralized exchange users are even at an advantage to simply withdraw their BNB to BSC using non-custodial wallets like Trust Wallet and MetaMask. PancakeSwap is also compatible with multiple wallets and it's preferred for its low fees. These low fees however, have attracted a few scammers to launch their projects on this DEX as not much vetting is done.

Trader Joe

Built onto the Avalanche ecosystem, Trader Joe is regarded as a one-stop DEX aggregator due to its ability to combine DEX services with DeFi lending to offer leveraged trading. Trader Joe offers products that are community-driven, allowing it to give fees collected through swaps and liquidation back to users. It facilitates this reward system through its native token JOE, a staking mechanism which also rewards its holders with a share of exchange revenues (Arti, 2021).

Trader Joe recently integrated with Autonomy network's (AutoSwap) DApp to provide limit orders and stop losses. This integration brought automated trading experience to Trader Joe's community, further increasing the already largest TVL for a DEX on Avalanche blockchain (Chainwire, 2022).

Raydium

Raydium is an AMM built on the Solana network with the purpose of facilitating easy swaps on the Serum DEX. Contrary to other AMMs that do away with order books, Raydium provides on-chain liquidity to a central limit order book. The deposited funds are then converted into limit orders recorded in Serum's order book in order to grant Raydium liquidity providers access to Serum's order flow as well as their existing liquidity (Arti, 2021).

CEX Versus DEX

Besides the obvious difference of centralization or decentralization, CEX and DEX also have distinct features that make them either favorable or unpleasant to use.

- One of the key features governing CEXs is that they are regulated, therefore, enforced by the law to comply with certain policies like those that govern traditional financial service providers. For instance, users of CEX platforms need to upload their identity documents and proof of residence (KYC) which can be such a pain to go through. The entire concept of decentralization is against this, as it advocates for anonymity and thus, saves the trouble of dealing with paperwork which then grants instant access to users. After connecting your wallet to a DEX, which can take a few seconds, you can start buying and swapping crypto right away without having to prove who you are or where you're from. With most CEXs, users are restricted from trading, funding, or withdrawing from their accounts unless they are KYC-verified, a process that is not only strenuous but irritating as well.
- Failing to comply with regulations can lead to a CEX being censored or closed down, while DEXs are censorship-free as they don't have any rules to follow, other than what the written code instructs. However, this feature makes trusting a CEX easy, knowing that it is regulated.
- DEXs are trustless because smart contracts are transparent and audited openly. There is no need to trust that an exchange would come out and declare bankruptcy while this is the case with CEXs, whereby you have to trust that the exchange has your best interests at heart, and that it is safekeeping your funds the same way you trust a bank. Not all CEXs reveal the entire audit results, raising questions that they're susceptible to misconducts.

- Regarding security of users' funds, CEXs are high risk as they keep custody of the funds, making them a target for hackers. Bitfinex being hacked billions worth of crypto in 2016 should have been enough evidence that scammers like to pull the biggest heist, with their focus being where funds are already pooled together, like in a bank. Crypto in centralized exchanges is the main target than a random individual wallet raid. Several exchanges continue to have their security compromised. Bitmart was swindled out of $100 million worth of mixed cryptocurrencies on the Ethereum blockchain and $96 million from Binance Smart Chain network (Thurman, 2021). There is no single point of failure when using a DEX, an attack is personal or targetted to you as an individual, as you only have the private keys to your wallet. If you safeguard your funds with strict security measures, then you should be just fine.
- CEXs are usually user-friendly with a great interface. They also have a number of preferred features like margin, futures, and spot trading as well as being able to set stop loss and take profit parameters. CEXs also grants users freedom and access to place limit orders at desired price levels. DEXs, on the other hand, have limited features and only allow instant execution of trades.
- Another pro for CEXs is the ability to trade using fiat, which is a great feature for beginners who are yet to acquire their first crypto. This is a major drawback for DEXs, as it means users still need to access CEXs to buy crypto and then move it to a DEX. DEXs only allow crypto for crypto swaps, not crypto for fiat or vice versa.

Stablecoins

Cryptocurrencies are known to be highly volatile instruments, and that has been one of the reasons that some investors want nothing to do with them. While that is true for most cryptocurrencies like Bitcoin and altcoins, there is a better alternative to the narrative. If you guessed fixed assets, congratulations. Stablecoins are cryptocurrencies that have a fixed value because they are backed by a fixed asset. Instead of their value being determined by supply and demand, stablecoins have their value pegged to the value of a real world asset that has its own value. For instance, assets with a peg to the price of gold, have their value in tandem with that of gold. This means that these assets do not have a fixed value themselves, but they will never be pricier or lower than the asset they are pegged to. If a coin is equal to an ounce of gold, no matter what happens to the price of gold, that coin will always be equal to an ounce.

How Do Stablecoins Work?

Instead of having a fixed supply like most cryptocurrencies, the supply of stablecoins increases or decreases depending on the value of their underlying asset (Tekeli, 2021). For example, if there were 100 USDT tokens in supply with a $100 value and the value of a dollar drops to $90, the supply of USDT tokens will also be reduced to only 90 tokens. Similarly, if the buying power of the US dollar increased to $110, the supply of USDT tokens making up that value would increase so that they always match.

This brings more trust in cryptocurrencies to people with low risk appetite as to them, it's like their money is still in the traditional finance system. They're rest assured that they will not wake up one day to their portfolio having dropped by 90% during the dip or miraculously having the value of their accounts rising to over 400%. Their portfolio will always be equal to that of the underlying asset. Therefore, stablecoins act as the best of both digital and physical worlds where users have an advantage of decentralization and a controlled value of their assets with auditing.

This would happen if all stablecoins were 100% backed by an asset they claim to be backed by, which can only be proven through auditing.

Currently, the value of stablecoins is based on the perceived value rather than inherent value, as proofing that the company actually owns the asset backing their stablecoin in the correct proportion is mysterious without auditing. Below we have different classes of stablecoins based on what assets they are pegged to.

Fiat-Backed

These are stablecoins that have their value pegged to that of a country's fiat currency. Several coins such as Tether (USDT) and USD Coin (USDC) are backed by the US dollar. eNaira has its value pegged to the value of the Nigerian Naira. Some stablecoins are backed by other nation's currencies, such as the Australian dollar or Euro.

This means one USDT token is equated to one US dollar. In a perfect world, this means that for every Tether token, Tether Limited, the company associated with Bitfinex, can prove that they have a real US dollar or fiat to back it. Speaking of an asset that occupies the number three spot by market cap, with almost $80 billion, that raises serious questions whether the company has $80 billion worth of hard cash in their reserve. But this is not the perfect world, and Tether's website shows that they are not 100% backed by US dollars but by Tether's reserves (Tether, n.d.).

Commodity-Backed

Commodities like gold, silver, iron, or oil have a unit of measure that is used to evaluate them such as an ounce or a barrel. Stablecoins that are backed by commodities have their unit of measure equated to the unit of their underlying commodity. As with fiat-backed stablecoins, proving that there are actual reserves of commodities backing these coins needs thorough auditing.

Take PAX gold for example, a stablecoin that claims it is entirely backed by gold at one PAX token redeemable for one troy ounce of a 400 oz London Good Delivery gold bar. This gold is supposedly stored in

Brink's vault. What would happen if all holders of PAX gold tokens redeemed their crypto for the real asset? Would everyone get their physical gold?

A German-based company, Karatbars, made the claim that their KBC coin was backed by real gold, but some users have not been able to redeem the gold that they bought with fiat. The KBC was delisted on CoinMarketCap in 2019 as it seemed that the coin was partially backed by gold, leaving those who invested with the mindset of owning gold high and dry as it plummeted in price prior to it being delisted on all exchanges, after the foundation was told to seize operations (Foxley, 2019).

Crypto-Backed

Some stablecoins are backed by one or more cryptocurrencies. Instead of the price of one coin being completely determined by supply and demand of that particular coin, the value of other coins associated with it is indirectly proportional to its value. DAI token is an example of crypto-backed stablecoins; it is also soft-pegged to the US dollar.

Algorithmic or Non-Collateralized Stablecoins

Non-collateralized stablecoins are run by an algorithmic code. While this type of stablecoins have endured their own set of shortcomings that are discussed below, the advantage of algorithm-run protocols is that they are completely decentralized, as opposed to the aforementioned stablecoins. This simplifies things as smart contracts are publicly accessible and easy to audit transparently if the assets are following the written code. There are three algorithms governing stablecoins.

Rebase

This type of algorithm is a self-run code where the smart contract knows when to increase or reduce the supply of tokens to ensure that the wallet balance reflects the same value as the invested currency. In this case, stablecoins are aware of their own price in such a way that whenever there is a mismatch, the algorithm automatically recalculates and the token balance of holders is increased to stay on par with the value of the underlying asset (Whiteboard Crypto, 2021a).

Token holders will each have their wallets topped up with the newly minted coins to ensure that their wallet balance stays the same value. The opposite action occurs when the value of the underlying asset decreases and the algorithm deducts tokens from each holder's wallet so that the token balance and the wallet value match. This is called debase, and just like rebase, tokens will automatically decrease irrespective of whether they are on an exchange or in a cold storage. Rebase and debase algorithms thus focus on supply volatility instead of price volatility to ensure that the value of stablecoins remains fixed to that of the underlying asset.

Seigniorage Supply

Seigniorage is the term that refers to the profit made from the difference between the cost of minting a currency and its face value, usually by governments or reserve banks (Sweta, 2022). Regarding stablecoins, this concept is used to incentivize token holders for keeping the price of a stablecoin equal to the value of its underlying asset. For instance, with Basis Cash, the stablecoin keeps its peg by using three types of tokens to keep its supply in check in the following manner: When the price of Basis Cash exceeds that of a US dollar, the price is pushed down to maintain the peg by increasing the supply of Basis Cash. The excess supply is then held through the second token where holders hold the new tokens in the form of Basis Shares (Coinmarketcap).

On the other hand, when the price of Basis Cash falls below that of the US dollar, the supply is reduced from circulation through the use of the third token, Basis Bonds, whereby holders of Basis Cash use the excess supply to buy Basis Bonds and are incentivized to do this. Although this was the initial plan according to what the pseudonymous founders, *Rick* and *Morty* claimed, things didn't work out that way. Like most seigniorage supply currencies, the price of Basis Cash and its sister tokens has fallen way below its intended peg in a death spiral. This happens when investors exchange their coins for other crypto, thereby leaving the total supply with excess and worthless coins, the doom faced by all three Basis tokens (Whiteboard Crypto, 2021a).

Empty Set Dollar is another seigniorage supply stablecoin that was launched with the intention to expand the work started by Basis Cash. With an anonymous founding team, no collateral, elastic supply, composability, and token-based governance, ESD painted a fantasy of true decentralization as these features, straight up, were meant to give centralized stablecoins a run for their money (Freiberg, 2020).

Slightly similar to Basis Cash, ESD offered a pair of tokens in the form of share stable coin and bond coin where users were rewarded for staking their ESD with income on the ESD prices over the US dollar. When the price of ESD falls below the US dollar, users can purchase coupons at a discount in order to get rid of any excess ESD stablecoins and simultaneously increase the price of ESD. Because of fear, uncertainty, and doubt (FUD), people tend to sell their coins for fiat, and this comes at no surprise that the intended ESD stablecoin has also failed to keep its peg when people pulled their funds and the value nose-dived (Whiteboard Crypto, 2021a).

Fractional Algorithmic Stablecoin

This is another algorithm used in stablecoins aimed at becoming a hybrid, whereby stablecoins are pegged to the US dollar with partial reserves in USD and another fixed asset. The one part fiat and one part other stable asset is the reason behind the name 'fractional'. A perfect example of the stablecoin that uses a fractional algorithm is Iron Finance which came with one token pegged to one USD in the proportion of 75% USDC and 25% titan. Similar to the examples above, the value of Iron

Finance stablecoin was adjusted to maintain its peg by means of allowing holders to help correct the price by means of incentives. Holders participated in arbitrage opportunities by buying and selling the newly minted coins or excess on the open market and redeeming them in part on the Polygon network as USDC and titan or on Binance Smart Chain as BUSD and steel.

If you guessed that Iron Finance also collapsed, high five! Prior to its crash, Iron Finance had performed exceptionally well as the total value locked increased from millions to billions in 2021 after its expansion to the Polygon network, as well as being endorsed by Mark Cuban. This saw the price of titan going parabolic from $10 to $64 (Finematics, 2021). After Cuban's recommendation that mooned the price, some users sold-off, bringing the price down, but the biggest crash was caused by the allowed arbitrage feature that users overused. Users saw opportunities to buy one of the pairing coins cheaper on one platform and sell them in Iron Finance. When whales took advantage of this opportunity, it confused the price oracles and the stablecoin lost its peg, resulting in the biggest bank run in DeFi when the masses sold and the stablecoin was not stable anymore. This resulted in the crash of Iron Finance, like with other algorithm-based stablecoins.

Credit and Insurance

Credit

Credit facilities offered over decentralized networks are one of the best services that DeFi has to offer. That instant cash, or in this case crypto injection, to take advantage of available opportunities and its effortless provision by DeFi lending platforms is causing disruption to traditional finance. Despite the challenges faced by the crypto industry, the integration of financial services into decentralized protocols has grown the total value locked (TVL), with smart contracts revolutionizing the loan system and threatening centralized financial houses (Dutta, 2021).

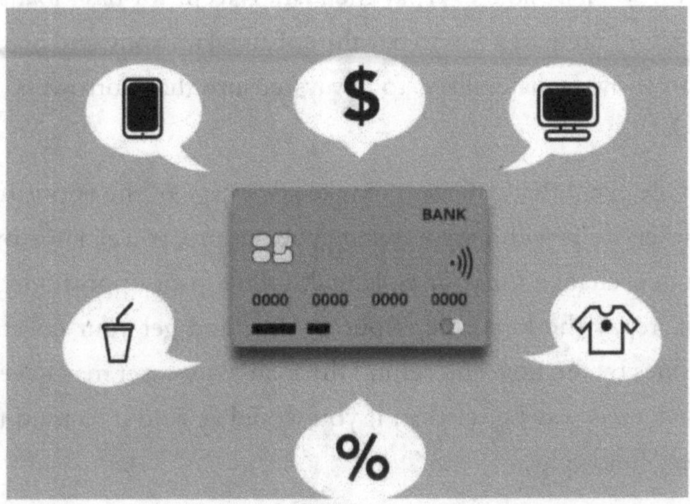

Some of the reasons DeFi has been well-accepted by the crypto community, is the ability for users from emerging economies—where accessing a basic banking profile can be a pain—to access any amount of crypto loan through a mere interaction with a smart contract. Accessing financial assistance and investing in lending and borrowing platforms has never been so easy without a governing intermediary.

Lending and Borrowing

The DeFi landscape is a growing niche, with most of TVL locked in lending protocols like AAVE, Compound Finance, and MakerDAO. The process of securing a loan from a traditional finance house is not easy, as it involves a lot of background checks, a must-have healthy credit score, and supporting documents like payslips or bank statements to indicate that you'll be able to repay a loan. Even after providing tedious paperwork, a bank might still decline to offer you a loan. But with DeFi protocols, there is no need to go through that long process just to borrow funds.

As long as you deposit collateral to a lending protocol, you receive your borrowed funds without a need to do a background check. In this trustless system, the only thing between you and your funds is a smart contract. You don't need to know who the borrower is, nor do they need to trust if you'll be able to repay the loan. Except for flash loans, securing a loan in DeFi requires you to pay the collateral upfront, and in most cases, the loan is overcollateralized to always ensure that borrowers' funds are secured.

In the event that you want to take advantage of the opportunities that the market offers without you selling your crypto, you can borrow another crypto in exchange for your collateral, follow your opportunity, cash out from it, repay the loan, keep your profits, and get your collateral back. Sometimes by the time you refund the loan, your asset may have grown in value, which is way better than if you would've sold it to fund the hunch you were following.

Insurance

The year 2021 alone saw over $1.2 billion in crypto hacks across five large projects! The Polygon network suffered the biggest dent with over half of that collective loss at $611 million stolen from it. Bitmart, a centralized exchange, comes second, losing over $196 million. Adding to that loss, Cream Finance, Vulcan Forged, and Badger Finance took the knock after hackers had their way with their crypto holdings (Dickens, 2021). These are just a few of the projects that experienced a loss in the decentralized world. In the past years, the losses have been even worse, and that's putting it lightly.

One of the most common financial services that makes traditional finance houses abundant wealth is insurance. That is because risk is everywhere, from arson, theft, unexpected deaths, terminal illnesses, and death from natural causes as well as natural and man-made disasters. Accidents happen everywhere, and if you're caught unaware, the impact can cause a serious dent to your finances, in addition to the event itself. To mitigate these risks, there are insurance policies that cover us from any disaster or any harmful event.

While insurance is a common service in the central world, the decentralized world is no different as it's even more prone to risks in a permissionless, ungoverned system where a lot of bad deeds go unpunished. A lot of people who are not keen to join the digital space hint at the risks involved that in the past were not financially catered for. As we've already covered, decentralization does not bring benefits only to good people, but the open-source code allows hackers and all bad actors alike. While the smart contracts are made public for the benefit of transparency, hackers have taken advantage and continue to use the provided information in a malicious way. The opening paragraph gives enough evidence that even the largest protocols, that you'd assume know better, dropped the ball and investors' funds were compromised.

Amongst many things that could go wrong in the decentralized world, smart contract failures, protocol attacks, exchange hacks, and stablecoin crashes pose a higher risk for the entire platform's failure and investors losing money, and faith in that platform. Of course, other events like an individual being hacked or losing their private keys, do happen from time to time, but mostly go unreported or disregarded as it doesn't involve many people like in the first instance. These turnouts of events led to DeFi insurance, which basically is buying coverage against losses caused by events in the DeFi industry.

Like with traditional insurance, you need to pay a premium in order to receive coverage over your crypto assets. For instance, if you want to cover your 100 BTC, you may be required to pay a yearly premium of 0.1 BTC, which is really not too bad considering that when you claim, a certain amount will be paid to you. You may be wondering how this works, reviewing the following protocols will shed some light. Decentralized insurance protocols rely on liquidity providers known as cover providers, who are investors who put their money in a smart contract-run DAO and earn yields for taking the risk. Cover givers are an important aspect to the whole concept as they also do things in a decentralized manner so that no one can run off with their money, or that no government can shut them down as would be the case with traditional finance.

Cover buyers, or policyholders need to claim when certain events that they paid to be covered for occur. But in DeFi, it happens in an effortless manner that would otherwise be hasslesome in the central world. DeFi insurance protocols use oracles, which are also smart contract platforms that are designed to obtain off-chain data and report it to the on-chain protocols. Oracles like Chainlink are able to track data in the real world, such as stock prices, sporting events results, or temperatures. For example, if you take out a policy that you want your investment in a new Web 3.0 company to be covered, oracles will track the performance of that company by analyzing stock prices, and will know when the company underperformed and you'll be liable to receive the cover for your loss. You won't have to provide redundant proofs for your claim to be accepted as is the case with some centralized insurances.

Cover suppliers, or insurance liquidity providers, are the ones who endure the most risk should the insured event take place and their pooled money gets to pay your cover. Unless the claims are from multiple cover buyers who experienced the same event that need to be compensated at the same time, the investment of the cover supplier is usually safe.

Nexus Mutual

Launched in July 2019, Nexus Mutual is one of the largest DeFi insurance protocols built on the Ethereum network. As an actuary scientist, the founder of this automated discretionary mutual boasts over 15 years' experience in the insurance industry. Nexus is a pioneer of decentralized insurance with the highest TVL, having rewarded early adopters and holders of the governance token with parabolic success. Although it's registered as a non-profit organization in the UK, it takes the DAO model that is governed by its members who get to vote on how it's run, what claims need to be paid, and how much premiums should cost (Knight, 2021).

With this DAO, cover buyers pay about 2.6% annually to cover their digital assets against a smart contract bug. Anyone can decide to become a cover supplier as this is in a decentralized Ethereum network. Nexus Mutual will then use the pooled funds in the form of ETH or NXM (the mutual's native token) to pay coverage when or if the bug has been discovered in the DeFi app. The running of this DAO is in the hands of its members who oversee key functions like risk assessment, claims assessment, capital provision, and overall governance based on votes.

Nexus offers a range of covers that the buyer can choose from, depending on how long they want cover for, the risk, and the type of asset they are using to pay their premiums. It allows premiums in ETH or NXM. The NXM token, which is the medium across the Nexus' ecosystem, is only accessible through the Nexus platform, where only KYC-approved members can hold it. However, a wrapped token (WNXM) can be accessed through most exchanges, both centralized and decentralized.

InsurAce Protocol

InsurAce is the first multi-chain DeFi insurance protocol that provides services and products across different networks to protect against risk and vulnerability in the decentralized world. As already mentioned, the blockchain industry is a risky niche that not only profits well-meaning people but bad actors alike. While Nexus Mutual is the pioneer in this decentralized insurance space, and thus trusted by the masses as evident with their TVL, it is limited to the Ethereum network. This means that some decentralized applications and smart contracts that are built on other blockchains like Avalanche, Binance Smart Chain, and Cardano, have limited to no coverage on Nexus Mutual. InsurAce protocol is the first one to offer insurance services to multiple networks.

InsurAce protocol provides decentralized cover against smart contract vulnerability, custodian service risk (from compromised central exchanges that hold your funds), and IDO risk. Oliver Xie, InsurAce protocol founder and project lead, told *CrowdFund Insider* that this protocol provides insurance services and products in a multi-chain environment including Ethereum, Binance Smart Chain, Heco, Polygon, Fantom, and Solana. Xie also confirmed that the protocol partnered with Elrond, which is a more-versed public chain, a partnership that enhanced the protocol's landmark in the public chain ecosystem (Faridi, 2021).

Besides the multi-chain environment, there are a few other features that make InsurAce shine in comparison to Nexus Mutual. Nexus only allows access to KYC regulation-compliant members, which is somehow a centralized feature. InsurAce on the other hand, requires no KYC and it can be accessed directly from a Web 3.0 wallet like MetaMask instead of requiring users to register for membership through their platform only; where they are even required to pay a small amount of ETH for membership fee. This makes the on-boarding process easier on InsurAce than on Nexus Mutual (The Babylonians, 2021).

Another upside is that InsurAce costs relatively low premiums, especially on bulk buys, and provides portfolio protocol underwriting, while Nexus provides specific protocol underwriting with high fees (no surprise as it's on the Ethereum network). Users can easily bundle protocols they want covered into one basket, something that would need to be done for every individual product on Nexus, paying ETH fees as many times as your products count.

There are currently three ways in which you can get involved with InsurAce: as a cover buyer, as an underwriter, or as an investor who believes in the native token (INSUR) that is a gem below $0.50, 97% down from its all-time high (ATH) of $15. And unlike NXM, INSUR can be found on multiple exchanges.

It is also worth noting that InsurAce is the new kid on the block, established in 2019 and having only launched in 2021; in March on Ethereum and June on BSC. InsurAce also has an experienced leading team, consisting of project lead, *Oliver Xei*, who is the former APEX CTO and founding member with experience in financial markets. It also consists of FinTech and digital assets tech lead *Sum Wei*, who has over 10 years' experience working with IBM and Microsoft, and marketing lead *Dan Thomson* who is a former *Goldman Sachs* and Cambridge graduate with over six years' experience in crypto. This shows that it's still in its infancy phase with a wider room to mature.

Opium.Finance

Opium.Finance is a different type of insurance from the ones above as it merges real world assets with decentralization. With RealT.co, which is a real estate tokenization system on the Ethereum blockchain, this protocol offers protection for no occupancy events. This means that it covers the loss that a real estate investor suffers when there is no tenant in the property they invested in. For investors who are a part of RealT.co, they expect to receive monthly rent for their property, which cannot be guaranteed as tenants can relocate anytime, or for some reason fail to pay rent, causing a dent to the property inventor's fund. To prepare for this, an investor can buy insurance from Opium.Finance, and pay a premium through a smart contract to get a tokenized position (like a derivative) for that fateful event.

During months of no occupancy or low rent, the smart contract automatically compensates the investor's balance. For example, if you expect $1,000 rent from RealT.co and for that month the tenant only stayed for two weeks and paid $500, the smart contract will pay you the remaining $500 so that your monthly rent is unaffected. It will even pay you a full month's rent in the event that you had no tenant for the entire month, or however long it takes (Opium.Finance, 2021). As we'll see with decentralized derivatives further in this chapter, Opium.Finance works in a similar manner.

The biggest risk here lies with the sellers of protection or stakers, because once a no occupancy event has occurred, they are not allowed to unstake their funds until there is a tenant. If there is no tenant for a prolonged period, stakers may lose all their collateral. Stakers can unstake on the first day of every month or they can stake their LP positions as ERC-20 tokens and their stake earns all buyers' premiums.

Investors and traders can find OPIUM token on exchanges like Gate.io, currently at around $0.50, its all-time low (ATL), and 97% down from its ATH of $23. Of course, one needs to do their own due diligence as to why the token dropped that low, whether it was REKT or if it still has potential. DeFi insurance is still at its infancy, with over $70 billion TVL in DeFi protocols, and less than 2% of it insured, opening a huge room for decentralized insurance coins to grow.

Asset Management, Lending and Borrowing

Asset Management

Asset management is a systematic approach and practice of optimizing total wealth overtime by acquiring, trading, and maintaining investments that have the potential to grow in value (Ganti, 2021). It's a way of diversifying your DeFi portfolio by considering what to bundle in your set to reduce the risks of investment. What you choose to add in your basket is totally up to you, your risk appetite, your choice of platform, with the assets at your disposal.

As with traditional asset management, DeFi asset management still needs proper allocation in relation to the risk you're willing to take on. You can build a diversified portfolio that is well-balanced with different asset classes or baskets of assets. With the help of Set Protocols, DeFi allows bundling of assets into different sets. For instance, you can allocate 25% of your portfolio for a set of oracles, 25% for a set of aggregators, 25% for a set of stablecoins, and the remaining 25% allocated to different individual assets. You can even have a set on top of another set that automatically rebalances your allocation of assets in your portfolio (CoinGenius, 2020).

The great thing about asset management on DeFi protocols is the ability to create hyper-customized portfolios that fit individual needs. With robo-advisors, you can have your portfolios rebalancing on their own without the need for you to check them all the time. You can have your yield farms, liquidity pools, and raids rebalancing according to the opportunities that are available at a time, all without you having to manually shift things around. Some aggregators like 1inch protocol allow you to optimize your profits by automatically switching across multiple DEXs and networks to find the best APYs.

DeFi allows so much freedom in comparison with traditional asset management. You can have your assets bundled and allocated according to your risk appetite, hedge your assets, and insure your smart contracts to mitigate some risks. The only time to check your device would be to harvest your farms, compound, or change your sets if you want to manually do that, or you can have these activities automated so that you can have more freedom and time to look for other opportunities. You can even use portfolio trackers so that you're updated with how your asset management is going and do minimal adjustments as it pleases you.

With decentralized apps, you can embed your life goals and allocate funds for them through asset management. With wealth calculators, you can preview how much you need to reach your goals, how long it will take to meet your solvable problems, or how you can collapse time with different activities bundled and automated for you. Bear in mind that DeFi is also liquid 24/7. You can decide to change your fund allocations as you wish, giving you flexibility that traditional asset management can never offer you, at least not without making you pay a hefty amount for it.

Decentralized asset management is giving traditional finance a run for their money. There's so much you can do at a fraction of a price. Asset managers and advisors generally charge an arm and leg to comprehensively create portfolios with growth, hedging, liquidity, and income, thereby raising the cost of asset management. Something that DeFi protocols can do in one transaction at relatively low fees. For instance, Zapper.fi (DeFiZap) introduced the ability to bring multiple positions, yield, risk management, and layering exposure in one zap (Menasakanian, 2021).

With evaluation of the risk profile and customized fit recommendations, this proves compatibility aspects of DeFi asset management. You can create a set on TokenSets or buy a set that matches your trading philosophy, and enjoy asset management on a trustless network. In fact, Set Protocols have tools for everyone, whether you're a developer, asset manager, or methodologist which can help you create, manage, and grow your set. Thus, asset management through DeFi has never been so simplified, flexible, and permissionless.

Derivatives and Lotteries

Derivatives

As the name suggests, derivatives derive their value from the price of an underlying financial asset such as a bond, commodity, stock, crypto, index, or another derivative. Traditionally, derivatives are commonly used on forwards and futures, which both entail contracts between a buyer and seller to trade an asset at a preset price at a date in future Forwards are privately negotiated contracts exchanged between traders and are obtained over the counter while futures are usually standardized contracts that are obtained through exchanges (Phung, 2019).

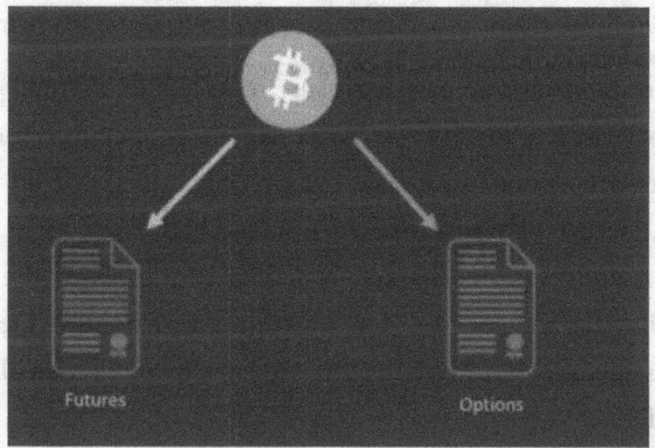

Forwards typically have more flexible terms and conditions than futures, and are thus widely used by most hedgers to avoid volatility of a price's asset. However, forwards are prone to counterparty risks whereby one party may default because they're handled in private. Futures contracts on the other hand are guaranteed to be settled as they occur over registered exchanges, which prevents defaulting of any other party. Most speculative traders use futures traders to scalp in the direction of the traded position.

Other common uses of derivatives include options and swaps. These can be conducted on trading platforms and decentralized exchanges. Unlike traditional derivatives that may take time to be approved and listed, anyone can create derivatives on DeFi and have access or provide liquidity right away.

Two main uses of derivatives are hedging and speculation. Traders use hedging to offset the losses that are involved with trading a direction that goes against their positions. This means that they trade the same pair but with different directions (selling and buying simultaneously) so that the winning trade offsets the losing trade and thus the trader ends up with profits or is protected from substantial losses. Yield farmers use hedging to offset impermanent loss when one of the tokens they've used to provide liquidity drops in value in relation to the one it's paired to.

Derivatives give an easy exposure to assets that would otherwise be hard to access. For instance, a trader can easily speculate the price of oil and either use options to call or put on oil futures, instead of buying or selling the actual oil barrels. Speculation and hedging work in sync as more liquidity is added to the market by speculators to assist the people who want to buy derivatives in order to hedge. Most popular DeFi derivative protocols include Synthetix, UMA, Hegic, Opyn, Perpetual, dXdY, and BarnBridge.

Synthetix

A brainchild of *Kain Warwick*, Synthetix boasts being the largest DeFi derivative protocol built on the Ethereum network. This DeFi protocol allows the creation of synthetic assets, which are financial instruments in the form of ERC-20 smart contracts that track the price of their underlying assets such as fiat currency, crypto, indices, and commodities. Holding these smart contracts, which are also known as 'Synths', grants the ability to track and provide returns of their underlying asset without the need for the user to hold that particular asset (Warwick, 2020).

Synthetic assets are based on overcollateralized debt pools whereby the trader must provide collateral and in turn, receive the Synthetix Network Token (SNX) which can be traded on decentralized trading platforms, such as Kwenta, dHedge, and ParaSwap. This means that for every $500 of collateral paid in the form of SNX, only $100 of it can be issued as Synths or the representative of the underlying asset. This is because the Synthetix derivative protocol is 500% overcollateralized (Finematics, 2021a).

Unlike with stablecoins whose value is pegged to the underlying asset and may be directly exchanged for that asset, Synths only expose the trader to the price of the underlying asset but it doesn't mean that the trader owns the asset. For instance, holding tokenized gold, PAXG, means that you actually own the gold equivalent to that stablecoin, which you can redeem through the holding company, Paxos. But owning Synthetix gold (sXAU) doesn't mean you can redeem it for real gold, but you can trade the price difference of gold, you simply have the exposure to make money through gold's price action.

Synthetic derivative protocols can be traded on most decentralized exchanges or decentralized apps because they are Ethereum-based. In order to accurately track prices of real world assets that are off-chain, price oracles such as Chainlink oracles are used to get off-chain feeds, or track the price of the underlying asset in real time and embed it on-chain.

Universal Market Access (UMA)

UMA is another Ethereum-based derivative protocol that allows creation of synthetic assets but without overcollateralization. Instead of using price oracles, UMA relies on liquidators who get a financial incentive for spotting and liquidating improperly collateralized positions. Besides proper collateralization, another difference between UMA and Synthetix is that UMA is regarded as the priceless derivative protocol. This is because UMA does not use price oracles, and thus has a wide list of derivatives that would be hard to track (Finematics, 2021a).

UMA challenges the use of price oracles with the theory that they can be corrupted, and to curb this, they fight to ensure that the cost of corruption is bigger than the profit from corruption (CoC>PfC). This encourages good behavior in a permissionless network where users would otherwise not be punished for malicious acting. According to one of the protocol's co-founders, Hart Lambur, UMA is aimed to serve as a major player towards more open, equitable, and sustainable financial markets. This is because anyone can access and create tokenized financial derivatives from anywhere in the world (Lambur, 2022). Through the use of the data verification mechanism (DVM), UMA token holders get to verify the price of synthetic assets and vote on it if there's a dispute, which means all along they strive to issue correct prices. Thus holding UMA tokens gives users governance, voting rights, and being paid for participation in the protocol.

Hegic

Created in 2020 by a pseudonymous developer, *Molly Winterminute*, Hegic is a protocol that allows traders to buy put or call options in a non-custodial, permissionless, and decentralized network. By incorporating specialized smart contracts, which in this case are referred to as hedge contracts, to traditional options trading, Hegic enables buyers or holders to buy or sell assets at predetermined prices known as the strike prices. Hedge contracts also give sellers known as writers the right to sell crypto assets during a certain time (Cryptopedia Staff, 2021).

Thus, the Hegic derivative protocol is an Ethereum-based on-chain option trading that provides functionalities beyond traditional financial derivatives. DeFi facilitates Hegic protocol's leveraged hedge contracts on assets like Ethereum and wrapped Bitcoin (WBTC) by use of liquidity pools. Liquidity providers earn rewards for depositing their funds into Hegic liquidity pools. Hegic users are able to protect the value of their crypto assets by hedging their investments. This derivative protocol also grants users the utility token, Hegic token (HEGIC), which gives them staking rewards and special benefits such as discounts when purchasing hedge contracts.

Opyn

A capital-efficient DeFi options protocol, Opyn was founded in 2019 by *Alexis Gauba*, *Aparna Krishnan*, and *Zubin Koticha*. It offers two types of options trading which allows users to earn ETH and ERC-20 tokens. Opyn V1 is designed to allow users to hedge the price movement of ETH in any direction. It later built its V2 on the Gamma protocol, which gives Europeans cash-settled options that auto-exercises upon expiry and creates new options on a whitelisted product (Crunchbase, n.d.).

With the Gamma protocol, users have the flexibility to reduce the amount of funds that want to lock in the system by creating spreads. And just like with V1, which is also known as Convexity protocol, users can create options tokens (oTokens) that represent the right to buy or sell certain assets at a strike price. For developers looking to build any application on top of Opyn, they do have a responsive discord channel (Gauba, 2021).

Perpetual Protocol

Originally known as Strike, Perpetual protocol was established in 2018 by *Yenwen Feng* and *Shao-Kang Lee* with the aim to curb exorbitant fees that are attached to the Ethereum network. Built on the Ethereum blockchain, this protocol uses virtual AMM (vAMM), which uses mathematical functions to determine the prices of tokens in order to provide instant swaps instead of using people or institutions that deal with order books to complete trades. This DEX does not allow spot trading, however, it offers leverage trading, short positions, and low slippage (price difference) (Bybit Learn, 2021c).

Perpetual protocol's governance token, PERP gives holders voting rights on the developments of the protocol. Holders can also stake their PERP to earn rewards in the form of newly minted tokens as well as a share on the platform's trading fees. Perpetual boasts having 24/7 liquidity throughout, and claims that there is no impermanent loss, which is a problem with most DeFi protocols. It has another upside of being highly secure, having been audited externally by reputable crypto auditors like ConsenSys and PeckShield, and received endorsement from both firms.

DXDY (dXdY)

Founded by a well-versed programmer and blockchain enthusiast, *Antonio Juliano* in 2017, dXdY is an open-source platform with smart contract functionalities designed to grant users crypto assets lending, borrowing, and trading opportunities. After raising over $10 million in seed venture capitalist funding, the dXdY platform went live in 2019, and hosted a successful ICO in September 2021 (CoinMarketCap, n.d.).

The governance token, DXDY, grants holders the ability to vote and propose changes on the Layer 2 protocol, as well as exposing them to great staking benefits and discounted fees. Built on Starkwire's StarkEx scalability engine, the Layer 2 scaling solution is designed to increase transaction speed and substantially reduce gas fees, and dXdY allows spot, margin, and perpetual trading on the protocol.

The protocol's users also have the benefits of having their funds accumulating interest as soon as they are deposited into the platform through the global lending pool. Borrowing on the platform also instantly exposes users to multiple assets available on the platform in exchange for their collateral in the form of assets in their possession. This collateral paid by borrowers guarantees the security of the lender's funds.

The dXdY protocol also embeds retroactive mining benefits in the platform to pay tribute to historical technology users by incentivizing them to trade on the effective and efficient Layer 2 protocol. It encourages this market participation through trading and liquidity provider rewards to users. For a coin that once reached an all-time high of $27.78 in September 2021 (during its ICO), some traders believe that dXdY is currently undervalued at less than $5.00, considering the fundamentals around this protocol; such as its $87 million 24-hour trading volume, and the fact that it's an active Layer 2 scaling solution (CoinMarketCap, n.d.).

BarnBridge

A risk tokenization protocol, BarnBridge allows hedging yield sensitivity and price volatility. It mainly exists to facilitate migration of yield-based derivatives from centralized systems to more efficient and risk-flexible decentralized financial systems. By matching supply with demand, it resembles UMA derivative protocol. Barnbridge applications, Structured Market Adjusted Risk Trenches (SMART) YieldBonds and SMART Alpha Bonds, function to aggregate buyers and sellers of risks by offering fixed and variable exposure to DeFi interest rates as well as dampened and levered exposure to price volatility respectively (BarnBridge, 2021).

Digital assets minted through BarnBridge can serve as collateral. DAOs govern BarnBridge on the Ethereum network by assigning the ERC-20 token (BOND) holders voting rights over decisions on how to utilize DAOs resources on the protocol. BarnBridge protocol makes it easy for DeFi users to invest by minimizing risk into divided pieces called trenches. This protocol is also running a liquidity mining program that distributes its governance token to users who stake stablecoins (Finematics, 2021a).

In their recent updates, BarnBridge announced that SMART Alpha has been integrated with Optimism, which is an Ethereum virtual machine (EVM) equivalent optimistic rollup chain that offers lower gas fees, lower latency, and greater throughput while also priding itself with world-class developer and a better UI. With its integration to Optimism, Synthetic, and Chainlink, BarnBridge protocol is cementing its position in the DeFi space (Dana, 2022).

Lotteries

DeFi just keeps getting better and better by offering traditional financial services in an improved manner that puts traditional finance institutions to shame. In a traditional lottery, people pool their funds together and the winner gets a huge sum of money when the odds favor them. For the lucky winner, their small investment has paid off, but for the losers, they can go on playing to lose (they get no refunds for playing). Thus, enriching others, especially the centralized authority facilitating this. This is not the case with the DeFi lottery. Here, players play to win and if they don't win, they get to keep their money to play again. In fact, I wouldn't even call it playing, because it's simply putting their funds in savings accounts on a decentralized, trustless protocol and just by doing that, they stand a chance to win the lottery.

PoolTogether

DeFi protocols like PoolTogether work like most decentralized staking platforms but it takes the staking to another level. What PoolTogether does is to allow users to stake their crypto to earn in a highly liquid platform where they can withdraw their funds instantly upon request. This protocol in turn leverages on other DeFi protocols like Compound and AAVE by lending the pooled funds to those protocols to earn interest that it will share with the members. The randomly selected winner of that day gets to win the interest made by the protocol on the secondary platform where it has loaned the pooled funds. Those who did not win, have not lost their funds as it would be the case with the traditional lottery system.

An open-source blockchain-based savings account that rewards users with prizes, PoolTogether aims at encouraging people to save money through its prize-giving model in the form of a decentralized lottery system. The protocol claims to have paid over $5 million in prizes, in the first two years of operating, with the highest paid winner receiving over $40,000 from initial deposit of $74 (Lightbulb Moment, 2021).

With the current interest rates for most US banks ranging from 0.01–0.05% per annum, DeFi protocols beat this as most have claimed to make more than 6.7% per month with protocols like PoolTogether. Users of the protocol claim that prizes are won daily, with a maximum of two prizes per a single wallet, granting equal winning exposure to the whale and the fish in the system (Defi Donut, 2021). While there are some risks involved with any financial system, which will be explained shortly, playing the lottery on DeFi has its great upsides. Your money is protected by smart contracts, which prevents the protocol from running off with investors' funds (or savers in this case). You'll recall that the smart contract is publicly accessible and can be audited to ensure its safety from hackers and freed of any bug issues.

Yieldly Finance

Another lottery protocol that has slightly tweaked the PoolTogether model is Yieldly Finance which was launched in June 2021. Unlike PoolTogether that is built on the Ethereum blockchain, Yieldly Finance is built on the Algorand network and is a native asset on Algorand's Layer 1. This protocol received mind-blowing reception and adoption when it reached $8 million TVL in 48 hours, the milestone that took giant DeFi protocols like AAVE and Compound a month to reach. A month later the protocol had locked over $23 million TVL between Algorand and Yieldy tokens (Nick, 2021).

Algorand holders typically earn staking rewards for simply holding ALGO in their wallets, but by putting down ALGO into Yieldly, holders forfeit these rewards, and instead are paid much better through the no-loss lottery protocol. In this protocol, holders earn about 22% APY in Yieldly tokens (YLDY), and furthermore, earn 102% for staking Yieldly. Bear in mind that these rewards refresh half-hourly and are redeemable daily due to the liquid market in DeFi, giving holders a decent portion of rewards without losing their initial ALGO investments (Nick, 2021).

Yieldly's founder and CEO, _*Sebastian Quinn,*_ made a bold statement that a no-loss lottery has the *"potential to become a major on-boarding platform* *into DeFi platforms at large"* (CoinTelegraph, 2021). Considering that Yieldly uses Algorand, a blockchain renowned for nominal fees, lightning-speed transactions, energy-efficient design, and being the go-to protocol to build a future-proof DeFi solution, there's a huge element of truth to Quinn's statement.

In addition to a successful hacker-resistant smart contract and blockchain audit by Halbron, an award-winning cybersecurity firm with the history of performing rigorous audits for blockchain giants like BlockFi, Coinbase, and Stellar, Yieldly also amasses endorsements from reputable supporters such as Borderless Capital, CMS Holdings, and OKEx Blockdream Ventures (CoinTelegraph, 2021).

Why No-Loss Lottery?

Lending protocols like AAVE start earning interest within 15 minutes of lending funds while Yieldly earns rewards half-hourly. This ensures that at the end of the day, the lottery platform has a lot of money to share with the randomly selected winners. Money that could be idling in your bank or any wallet, stands a chance to earn returns through the lottery protocol, while ensuring that you don't lose because you did not win the lottery.

The major downside is that of the protocol dependency risk, which means that the failure of one of the protocols that are key generators of daily interest like AAVE and Compound, would negatively affect the lottery protocol, because it would also lose members' funds which are invested in the failing protocol. However, bear in mind that the lending protocols like the ones mentioned here are also controlled by the smart contracts, which means that any risks are likely to be spotted and vetted early on. Another comfort is that some of these lending protocols are non-custodial, which means that the funds don't necessarily need to leave the lottery protocol's wallet. So the failure of the lending protocol might not be the end of the lottery protocol, but a serious cutdown to members' prizes while the protocol seeks alternative cash cows.

It's arguable that this is not like traditional lottery where players stand to win huge prizes from minimum investments in the form of lottery tickets, but DeFi lottery teaches people the habit of saving by incentivizing it. While the money you used to buy the lottery ticket is non-refundable in the traditional lottery system, DeFi protocols are highly liquid, which allows you to access your money anytime you wish.

Ethereum, Ether, Gas

Ethereum

Ethereum is a decentralized programmable blockchain that allows developers to build anything atop of it (Ethereum.org, n.d.). Founded in 2015 by a group of developers led by the Russian-Canadian *Vitalik Buterin*, this world-class developers hub is home to many DApps that bring countless solutions and improve on the limitations of the preceding blockchains like Bitcoin. Having co-founded Bitcoin Magazine at such a tender age could have been one of the reasons that Buterin had an upper hand to improve on Bitcoin's innovation in creating Ethereum. Unlike its predecessors that were focused on decentralized global payments or file sharing, Ethereum does a lot more, by providing developing tools to anyone who would like to build anything, including their own blockchain, application, currency, or game.

Ethereum currently uses the PoW consensus mechanism to validate the blockchain activities, but it is meant to upgrade to Ethereum 2.0 in the near future, which will use a more efficient, speedy, cost-effective, and environmentally friendly PoS. It has been one of the most profitable cryptocurrencies to mine although rewards have started to decline significantly (Spagnolo, 2022).

The list of possible applications that can be built on the EVM is endless. Smart contracts, DEXs, DAOs, and NFTs thrive on the Ethereum network. This makes this blockchain one of the largest and trusted decentralized networks that provide building blocks to take blockchain technology to another level. Replacing centralized servers with thousands of nodes run by developers and volunteers across the world is one of the reasons why Ethereum is regarded as the world's computer (Hertig, 2021).

Ether

Ether (ETH) is the native coin on the Ethereum blockchain. Without ether, navigating through the Ethereum blockchain is impossible as it powers every activity and operation on this network. Whether it's sending funds across different wallets, building an application, swapping, or minting NFTs, every transaction on the Ethereum network needs the user to have some ETH before it can be successful. This does not mean that ETH is required for all blockchains that are built on top of it. Yes, the process of creating a DApp will require one to have ETH for gas fees, but using that DApp doesn't necessarily need ETH, but gas fees in its native token. Ether is the second largest crypto by market cap, after Bitcoin.

With the long-term vision of Ethereum aimed at powering transactions beyond the financial landscape, allowing developers to build any DApp with unique functions, it handles more transaction volume than other digital assets. It also plays a huge role in DEXs, giving users exposure to different financial services without a central authority (Hertig, 2021). The main difference between Ethereum and ether is that Ethereum is the entire blockchain while ether is the native token that powers every transaction handled on the Ethereum blockchain.

Unlike most cryptocurrencies like Bitcoin, which has a hard cap of 21 million, ether does not have a hard cap; therefore, its supply will always increase. This feature is what makes the likes of Cardano, which is a PoS-using blockchain created by one of the Ethereum founders, *Charles Hoskinson*, and designed to have 45 billion maximum supply and ability to support DApps and smart contracts, to be the biggest threats to ether's future value (Miracle, 2021). That's because cryptocurrencies with a hard cap are deflationary, but ether, just like fiat, has its supply with no limit, which can lead to loss of buying power over time. With the implementation of the most-anticipated Ethereum 2.0 (ETH 2.0), these threats are highly controversial as its possibilities make it just as competitive.

Gas

Just like your car needs gas to move from one place to another, crypto transactions need to be fueled. Gas is thus one of the important components that power the blockchain network. Technically speaking, gas is the unit that measures computational effort required to execute any operation on the Ethereum network (Richards, 2022). Gas is measured in Gwei, whereby 1 Gwei is equivalent to 0.000000001 ETH, with wei being the smallest unit of ether. Think of wei as something similar to Bitcoin satoshis or fractions of Bitcoin.

You've probably heard of extortious fees on the Ethereum network, but I'll make that clear as to what causes fees to be high or low. Gas transaction fees are usually fixed depending on the type of transaction. For instance, you need 21,000 gwei to send any amount of crypto from one wallet to another, or 400 gwei to check the balance of someone's wallet. The gas price is the variable that determines the actual cost of gas fees. Multiplying the gas cost by the average price of gas results in the true cost of transacting on the Ethereum network. The average price of gas will change depending on the network congestion and the price of ether. Thus, the formula to calculate gas fees is like this:

Total gas fee = Gas unit (limits) x (Base fee + priority fee [tip])

Depending on how fast you want your transaction verified on the blockchain, you will either choose to pay low fees and settle for delayed transaction verification, or pay more gas to have your transaction prioritized on the blockchain. That's because miners will naturally choose to prioritize to validate the transaction of the one who pays more, because that's how they make money.

Some hacks to paying low gas fees include waiting for when there is less blockchain traffic to make your transaction, with weekends being some of the best times. If your transaction is not time-sensitive, you can withhold it until there are less people using the blockchain. You can also set a maximum gas limit that you're willing to pay, with which after your transaction has been executed, the Ethereum blockchain will refund the unused gas to your wallet. This helps to ensure that you don't unnecessarily cast out a transaction that ends up failing because you limited your gas fee. If a gas fee is too little, your transaction will fail to execute but you'll never see your gas fees again!

Ask the people who have tried to mint, collect, or swap NFTs; it can be a pain. You're not even entitled to claim those fees of a failed transaction because miners who validate the blocks still went out to work and thus, and earned those fees as rewards to determine whether to validate that transaction or not. Another gas fee hack is opting to use Layer 2 scaling solutions such as Arbitrum, dXdY, and Loopring, which are extension tools that aim to speed up the number of transactions that can be verified per second. Layer 2 scaling solutions, which are able to work off-chain and get verified on-chain, also help to significantly reduce block congestion in the Ethereum network (Mcshane, 2022).

Yield Farming and Liquidity Mining

Looking to make passive income with your crypto? Yield farming and liquidity mining might be your best bets! These two are closely related, so let's start with liquidity mining. Liquidity means the ease at which one asset is exchanged into fiat or another crypto asset. It is usually determined by availability of matching buyers and sellers willing to exchange assets within the same market. Some assets are highly liquid, meaning everytime you want to buy or sell them, you instantly get a willing seller or buyer. In the CEXs, this is easily visible through order books that record the amount of assets being traded, and the price that the buyer is willing to pay or the seller is willing to accept.

For instance, a buyer may want to pay 200 USDT for 0.07 BTC while the seller wants 250 USDT for that amount of Bitcoin. One of these parties will have to compromise depending on their matter of urgency. The buyer may decide to be patient and wait for the seller to reduce the price, or for another seller that will match their price. If no one is budging, that means there is less liquidity, and both parties may wait longer until their offers are matched. Traders take advantage of this by setting limit orders, which are orders that will execute when their desired price is triggered. The difference between the ask and the bid price is called the spread in CEXs, and that's how the exchanges also make money, besides the fees. This is similar to slippage in DEXs, which is the difference between the listed price and the actual price at execution.

To ensure that there's enough liquidity in DEXs, the concept of liquidity providers was birthed. This is whereby users who have their funds idling in their wallets, decide to provide liquidity for certain pairs to ensure that it is easy to exchange those assets. That means liquidity providers use their funds to provide equal value of two assets and lock it up in exchange for a reward. Traders or borrowers that are using the exchange to swap their tokens or acquiring loans pay a fee or commission, and this fee is what the exchange shares with everyone in that liquidity pool. So liquidity providers earn pool rewards for locking their crypto into a liquidity pool.

The pool rewards are either in the same currencies that the liquidity providers provided or in a different asset. Usually, liquidity providers receive LP tokens, which are redeemable for their supplied tokens when they want to stop providing liquidity, or they can use the LP tokens to trade other assets while their supplied tokens are earning rewards. Liquidity providers can also choose to stake their LP tokens into a farm where they will receive even more rewards, with compounding interest. That is where yield farming comes in, although sometimes the terms are used interchangeably. Yield farmers are basically liquidity providers that have staked their LP tokens into farms to earn even more rewards. Farmers can harvest their profits on a daily basis depending on which farms they are using, and they can lock those rewards in single pools or raids so that they get more of that locked asset, or a different asset. Thus liquidity mining and yield farming is a way to make money with less movements like trading.

Automated Market Makers (AMMs)

The scenarios that we've just explained above are made possible because of AMMs. To remove order books that record bid and ask prices, DEXs use AMMs which determine the prices of assets based on their supply and demand. AMMs are the reason liquidity pools exist and the reason why swapping tokens is made easy by liquidity providers. AMMs use a constant product formula to determine the price of tokens. While there are several mathematical formulas that can work out this, AMMs use the one proposed by Ethereum founder _Vitalik Buterin_:

$x * y = k$

Where x is token A balance, y is token B balance, and k is the constant balance or the unchanging value of between two tokens (Cryptopedia Staff, 2021a).

For example, to create liquidity for USDT/ETH an LP needs to provide equal value of both these tokens; $2,000 worth of liquidity can be divided into $1,000 for USDT and $1,000 for ETH. Then if the AMM says the initial rate of exchange between these two tokens is 1:1, and that multiplying them should always give the same product, in this case $1,000,000, this means that no matter which token supply increases or decreases, multiplying these two assets must always yield $1,000,000. To obtain this constant result, it means that the 1:1 ratio is variable and one asset may be more expensive than the other depending on its supply in the liquidity pool (Whiteboard Crypto, 2021b).

That is what determines the price of each token in the liquidity pool, and hence there is no need to have an order book. This constant formula ensures that the liquidity pool yields the same result. The more ETH is bought, the higher its price will be and the lower USDT will become in that particular pool. Arbitrage traders also take advantage of this information by checking which pools have a variable price than other exchanges, and thus they buy one asset on one liquidity pool and sell it in another to profit from price deviations.

Chapter 4: Investor's Guide to Digital Gold

The DeFi Marketplaces

Instead of using centralized marketplaces that are controlled from one access point, the rise in the use of DApps is a new trend. Crypto marketplaces allow users the flexibility of dealing directly with each other without intermediaries, which usually cause delays in productivity while also causing unnecessary exorbitant charges. As we already know, there is a lack of transparency in centralized platforms. Even those that are audited still have discrepancies that are hidden, only to blow up in the faces of users when it's already late to do any damage control. But with decentralized platforms, on top of not having to trust anyone, every move is recorded on the blockchain, so there are no surprises. When something fails, smart contracts are programmed to handle it. In this section, we'll look at some of the best DeFi marketplaces, but first let's see the weaknesses of centralized marketplaces.

First of all, there is usually a lot of red tape involved in centralized marketplaces for customers and for developers alike. There are tons of regulations that hinder true freedom in how a platform must run, to the finest detail of dictating the products and services that can be accessed through a marketplace. Centralized marketplaces pose the threat of censorship and halting of services should one party fail to comply with regulations. This usually affects others who have nothing to do with flawed regulations.

There is also a possibility of failure due to anything concerning the main team, this makes centralized marketplaces unsustainable and high risk. One of the reasons Bitcoin is still standing today is because Satoshi did not make it an individual's thing, with the intention that it runs smoothly without relying on one person or one organization to man things. The same applies with Etherum-based marketplaces. Whatever happens to Ethereum's founders or the marketplace founders will not affect the future of those platforms. Something that is community run operates at grassroots level, letting the community guide the market, and not the other way round. This has been the case with most online games whereby one kill switch affects other players with their accumulated levels (Hurley, 2015).

Centralized markets are usually an easy target for the bad guys because it's a known case that they keep records of their users. Because users are expected to comply with KYC regulations, centralized markets are the depository of tons of individual's identity and financial records. Hackers know the importance of gaining access to this classified information and thus, target centralized markets. This is what happens when you trust that someone will keep your information private and yet it gets in the wrong hands like when AWS leaked sensitive data (Pham, 2018). That's the reason why the trustless feature of decentralized platforms is a safer option.

One of the early examples of decentralized marketplaces that pioneered this prior to DeFi is none other than OpenBazaar. Created by the OB1 team in 2o14, this decentralized eBay version was a marketplace for almost anything anyone would want to buy on an online store with ease (Ivan, 2020). OpenBazaar accepted payments in over 50 cryptos including Bitcoin, Ethereum, and the privacy crypto, ZCash. This marketplace existed when a lot of people still found decentralization a mystery, and hence it did not get much anticipated clientbase which led to it closing down. But the users only had the good things to say about it (CoinDesk, 2021).

OpenSea

With the exponential rise in NFTs in this era, OpenSea marketplace is currently the number one decentralized marketplace for NFTs. It is built on the Ethereum network and is currently incorporated with Polygon blockchain and Klaytn network to give users choice of speed of access, competitive gas fees, and a wide range of items.

Created by *Alex Atallah* and *Devin Finzer* in 2018, OpenSea boasts of being the most trusted marketplace with endorsements from key players like Coinbase, Trust Wallet, and Founders Fund. OpenSea has a great UI, allowing users to only connect their crypto wallets and start browsing, minting, or collecting NFTs with ease.

Particl

The brainchild of *Ryno Mathee*, Particl is a decentralized peer-to-peer marketplace offering a variety of goods just like eBay or OpenBazaar. With no user data required to transact or stored on the server, Particl happens to be one of the safest marketplaces where users can choose to use the native privacy token PART or ShadowProject (SDC), where PART is hard forked from (Ivan, 2020). Merchants and users can easily download the desktop version and create a wallet within this marketplace. There is no need to connect your main wallet because you can swap only the amount you want to spend on the marketplace into the native token. PART transactions are completely anonymous, ensuring full privacy. Another key feature that makes PART a desirable token to transact with is that it is atomic compatible, meaning that it can be transferred amongst users without having to go through an exchange.

iExec

iExec is the newest kid on the block that uses a proof-of-contribution (PoCo) consensus mechanism protocol which is designed to provide trust in an open and decentralized environment of untrusted machines. This protocol also ensures that payments are always timely and fair. iExec is a decentralized marketplace for computer systems, servers, applications, and datasets where users can interact with other developers and exchange computing tools in a safe and private platform. iExec is a unique market network where developers, providers, and token holders can monetize their computing assets (iExec, 2022).

With this internet infrastructure feature, dataset, application, and computing resource providers can sell or rent their computing assets to other users. Then they can get paid on a pay-per-task model through the blockchain. With iExec oracle ecosystem, users will earn RCL tokens by providing specific oracles to available DApps. We don't know what's the future for this marketplace, but its mapped out vision and the interaction they receive on their GitHub page is promising and well anticipated by the community (Jacquot, 2022).

How to Invest in DeFi

This section is importantly articulated to give you a clear guide on where to start investing in DeFi. We will tackle a step-by-step process of getting started with recommendations of best wallets to choose from and renowned DeFi platforms that offer better annual percentage yield as well as greater user experience.

Selecting a Wallet

You need a decentralized wallet to invest in DeFi, because why would you want to use credit or debit cards? The main reason is to stay under the radar and unreliant to traditional financial institutions as much as possible. Below are properties and features you need to consider when selecting a wallet.

Accessible

You need a wallet with a great UI that you can access from any website or device. It must be a Web 3.0 wallet that can be interoperable from different sites at any given moment. Decentralized wallets can be accessed from multiple sites without the need to transfer funds for another site, you can literally do multiple transactions from one wallet. For instance, you can access your wallet to farm on several blockchains, to pay or send crypto to any other wallet using a different blockchain, link it to a decentralized marketplace, and hold different asset classes with different token standards all in one wallet.

Non-Custodial

Custodial wallets are the ones that are linked to exchanges whereby you entrust them to safeguard your funds. Even in the case where you misplace your password, these exchanges can help you to reset it because they store the main keys to your funds. That makes them no different from traditional intermediaries. And often, you are required to provide KYC documents which really is what DeFi is against. With non-custodial wallets, only you have access to your private keys, making you your own bank. If you lose your keys no one can help you to recover or reset your deleted or lost keys. You are responsible for the security of your own funds.

Key-Based

All DeFi wallets use private keys, usually a unique set of words called a seed phrase. There are no emails and mnemonic passwords that you need to input, only that randomly generated seed phrase that you got when you created a wallet. When backing up your wallet, ensure that the seed phrase is copied as is, without rearranging words. No one can help you if you lose your seed phrase. With a seed phrase, you can easily import your wallet on different devices.

Compatible

DeFi wallets are Web 3.0 wallets which are compatible with all decentralized applications, making it easy to navigate through DApps without having to leave the app. Once you're on a DApp, it automatically asks you to connect to a wallet. It will pick up the one you use frequently, or you can connect a new one. Some wallets have a desktop browser extension.

MetaMask Wallet

MetaMask is one of the best Web 3.0 wallets that is compatible with most DApps, making it easy to navigate between different blockchains using one device. You can easily have Ethereum-based assets in the same wallet as the Binance Smart Chain or Fantom Networks. It started as a web browser extension but now users can get the mobile app for convenient transacting from anywhere on this user-friendly wallet.

MetaMask is also ENS compatible, meaning that users can link a human-readable address like *anmera.eth* instead of having to double or multiple check that the random address is correct. Another great feature is that you can power up your congested transaction by adding more gas to make it a priority on the blockchain. You can also have access to multiple wallets and different ERC tokens without a need for another app.

Coinbase Wallet

Created by Coinbase exchange, Coinbase Wallet is a non-custodial wallet where private keys are not stored on the exchange but directly on your device. Coinbase Wallet is not the same as the application built-in wallet that comes with the exchange, usually called Coinbase Consumer, where a user can trade cryptocurrencies. While it's possible to store crypto on Consumer Coinbase, bear in mind that it means Coinbase is the primary custodian of your assets, but when your crypto is held in Coinbase Wallet, you have full custody of your assets. If you don't have your keys, then it's as good as not owning those funds. Coinbase Wallet is in your control; you own the funds in that wallet. Even when in unfortunate cases there is a hack on the exchange, Coinbase Consumer, your funds are not at risk because yours are held in a private wallet.

With Coinbase Wallet, users can access emerging Web 3.0 applications and store most assets including bitcoin, ether, other ERC-20 tokens as well as NFTs. Coinbase Wallet can be accessed on mobile devices or from a browser extension, allowing users easy access to Web 3.0 applications on desktop. You can have easy access to decentralized apps. Even with Compound you can automatically authorize your wallet and start borrowing and lending directly from your Coinbase Wallet. Coinbase Consumer clients can link their accounts with the Coinbase Wallet for seamless transfers, leveraging the on and off ramps that the exchange offers while being sole custodians of their funds.

In terms of UI, Coinbase Wallet still lacks a few integrations with other DApps. Unlike with other wallets like MetaMask, Argent, or Binance's Trust Wallet, Coinbase Wallet users still have to rely on Coinbase Consumer to trade their assets as it is not yet fully integrated to handle trades.

Argent

While there are several other non-custodial wallets like Binance Smart Chain Wallet, Trust Wallet, Atomic Wallet, Brave Wallet, and Wallet Connect, most of the features are pretty much similar to or between MetaMask and Coinbase wallets. The game changer and one of the most innovative wallet solutions comes in the form of a smart contract wallet or smart wallet called Argent, which is perfect for beginners and advanced users alike. Argent leverages the smart contract features with a great UI where the funds are held by the smart contract while private keys are stored on the users' device (mobile phone used to create the wallet).

Argent removes the complexity and overwhelming nature of users having to safeguard their assets with a paper backup and encrypted addresses. It is ENS compatible, making it easier to have easy to remember human-readable addresses. Users can create simple mnemonic addresses instead of using cryptic wallet addresses that need effort in double or multiple checking when transacting.

Argent wallet has a great UI, making it more preferred by beginners in the crypto space. It is a non-custodial wallet in that Argent does not store user's private keys but the mobile device acts as a custodian. Users can assign guardians in the form of trusted devices to help them to recover their accounts in the event that they lose their seed phrases or lose access to their main devices.

One of the key features of this wallet is that users can set a limit of daily withdrawals, a safety feature in the unfortunate event where if hackers gain access to the wallet, they cannot clean you out in a single transaction. This means that you can keep minimal withdrawal limits on a day-to-day basis and only increase them when you are moving lumps sums.

The cherry on top feature for this wallet is that it is gasless, meaning that there is no need to have Ethereum or BNB to power transactions. It offers free transactions, making it indeed a real paradigm shift in DeFi! Additionally, Argent has integrated most DeFi platforms like Compound and MakerDAO, simplifying DeFi lending and borrowing of funds on these protocols as well as giving sophisticated users access to explore a range of cryptocurrencies through Kyber Network (Campbell, 2022).

While Argent has a great UI with Venmo-like capabilities, security features, and integration with DeFi applications, it is important that this new kid on the block does not support a range of blockchains as it is an Ethereum-only wallet. However, it can store wrapped assets which are ERC-20 tokens fully collateralized by underlying assets.

After you have selected a wallet that you prefer, the next step is to fund it with crypto which you can access from CEXs (where if you're a beginner you can even buy straight from your bank card) as previously mentioned. Once you have funds in your MetaMask, Argent, Coinbase Wallet or any that tickles your fancy, you can go to decentralized protocols to provide an income-earning service as described below.

Four Ways to Invest in DeFi

Lending

This one feature is the main reason why DeFi could see the traditional banks suffering: Ease of access to loans with no excessive paperwork. With traditional finance models, we already said that you would have to have a good credit score to borrow money, which in general reduces the number of people that qualify for loans. Great news is that the number of people rejected by central financial institutions are now flocking to decentralized finance where their background or income scale does not matter.

As a lender, you can make money by locking your crypto in DeFi lending platforms and be paid interest. Borrowers are more than happy to pay this interest because of the benefits they gain from borrowing. Smart contracts then distribute accrued interest to lenders in proportions of funds they locked in. Lending is one of the safest ways to make money with DeFi as the money is guaranteed to be paid through fees that borrowers encounter to access loans. This happens because borrowers are charged prior to getting access to loans and in most protocols they are overcollateralized, which means they pay more than what they want to borrow. In the event that the market of the collateral crashes below the threshold, the protocol automatically sells the borrower's funds in order to pay the lenders' funds through a process known as liquidation. This is what ensures that the lenders' funds are safe (Prusso, 2021).

Overall, the lending process is a walk in the park in comparison with sitting with your bank manager in a boring and lengthy meeting where they explain your interest rate, that is a rip off of what you would in turn pay them if the tables were reversed and they were lending you money instead. Once you have chosen the DeFi platform to earn passively from, you just connect your wallet (which has your funds) to the platform and choose to lock your funds in there. You will already see the possible returns through a displayed APY. Once you click 'Stake', the rest is history; you will start earning interest as borrowers interact with the protocol.

The whole process can be done in less than five steps, and the great thing about lending on DeFi platforms as opposed to banks or investment institutions is that whenever you want access to your funds back, you can do that with a click of a button, choose to unstake and voila, you can withdraw or change lending platforms as you please! Better returns, great UI, no need to trust anyone, permissionless, what could be better?

Staking

Staking or PoS is the process of locking your crypto in an exchange for the following reasons. To earn staking rewards, duh! Okay, let's put it this way: This form of consensus algorithm is another way of creating blocks that create new crypto while validating transactions on the blockchain. Unlike PoW consensus that uses mining power from hardware, which is not only expensive to keep a miner as it consumes excessive energy, it's also bad for the environment due to the emitted carbon. An efficient way to validate transactions and introduce new coins to the market was thus formed and you guessed it, it's staking. With mining, miners compete to create a block and normally the one that has more hash power or those that combine powers in mining pools gets to create the block first and the mining reward (Prusso, 2021).

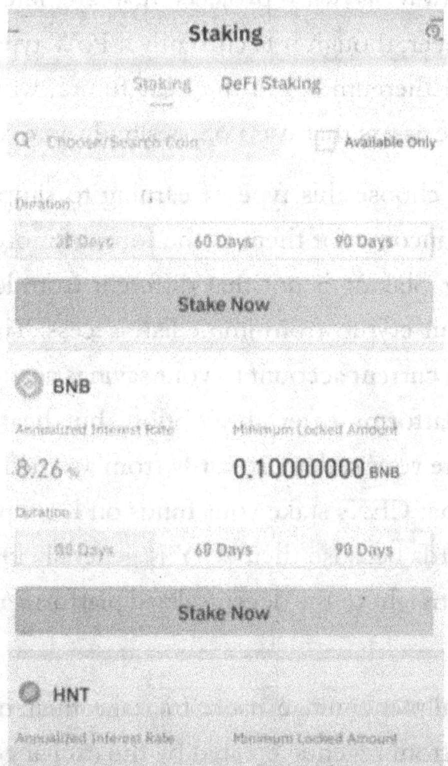

With staking, validators of transactions are chosen based on their stake, or the number of locked coins. The more coins are locked, the more weight you carry as a voter to decide which block gets created first, and hence the better the staking rewards. This algorithm is a more preferred way to validate transactions and bring new crypto because it is generally cheaper. There's no need for expensive hardware that does not guarantee rewards, instead, you can buy crypto which will earn two incomes: One in staking rewards and another as the value of that particular crypto increases. It is also environmentally friendly.

Now you know where staking is from but you may be confused by coins that you know that use PoW consensus like Bitcoin and Ethereum. Well, staking bitcoin on exchanges does not mean that it is a PoS type of asset, designed to be mined only through PoW, but exchanges reward you for locking it away as with projects that are intended to be staked. Ethereum however, though it is currently a PoW type of asset, it is being integrated into Ethereum 2.0 in the near future, which will use PoS. So staking, for these assets that use PoS, is simply an overlapping of a term.

Most users choose this type of earning to simply hold their crypto and it generates income for them in the form of more of the same crypto they are holding. Staking is not that different from lending as it involves locking away your crypto from immediate access. Think of moving your funds from your current account to your savings account. Both CEXs and decentralized platforms offer this option, but bear in mind that with CEXs, they share your staking rewards from accrued income with you. It is highly likely that CEXs stake your funds on DeFi platforms and simply share your rewards because their APY is generally lower than you would get if you went straight to the decentralized platform and earn your staking reward as is.

DEXs usually encourage users to stake their native token to earn shared rewards from revenue created by the exchange, say in the form of trading fees or from liquidity pools. With DEXs, it's even easier for users as they don't need to change their crypto to another like they would with lending above. DeFi protocols still offer better APY though, so it is totally up to you. Just as with lending protocols, you can unstake your funds any time you want, bearing in mind that locked staking for longer periods yields more staking rewards than flexible short-term staking.

Best Crypto to Stake

Based on fundamentals surrounding the following coins, their market capitalization, trading volume, ease of staking, availability on multiple exchanges, and average rate of return, the following coins made it to this list (Harshman, 2022):

- Ethereum (ETH)
- Binance Coin (BNB)

- USD Coin (USDC)
- Solana (SOL)
- Cardano (ADA)
- Polkadot (DOT)
- Avalanche (AVAX)
- Polygon (MATIC)
- Algorand (ALGO)

Becoming a Liquidity Provider

On CEXs, there is a need to keep order books as there aren't always an equal number of buyers matching sellers at a particular time hence there are different offers for buy and sell orders. Exchanges make money through these spread values or differences between ask and bid offers. This is why it takes longer for trades to be executed on CEXs because there are not always instant sellers matching buying offers. But that is also how traders make money, by looking at the order book to place their limit orders and also setting their take profit parameters to execute when the price on the order book is reached. While this might benefit savvy traders, beginners often don't have the patience to wait for an order to be fulfilled and choose to make an instant execution, which the exchange quickly allows that trade and simultaneously places another trade per the order book and make profit from covering the spread.

DEXs however, use liquidity pools to ensure that there are always matching sellers to buyers. This ensures instant swaps at a fee, of course. DEXs do this with the help of AMM protocols that are explored in Chapter 2. Liquidity pools are made up of equal value of token pairs. For instance, if you want to provide liquidity for the BTC/USDT pool, you can contribute $2,500 in BTC and $2,500 in USDT, totalling $5,000 in liquidity. By locking these assets in this manner, you will in turn receive LP tokens that represent your share in the liquidity pool and also that you will use to redeem your stake when you wish to. When you redeem your tokens, you will get your locked tokens in BTC and USDT equal to the LP tokens plus your share of the revenue (swapping fees that the DEX charges traders). Thus, becoming a liquidity provider earns you income passively, and is an easy way to invest in DeFi.

Yield Farming

Yield farming is another incredible way to make passive income on DeFi. It's basically an extension of being an LP. Instead of redeeming your LP tokens, you can place them into a farm where they will earn more of the same token or another token specific to that farm. It's a way of increasing your bag on a particular coin that you're providing liquidity for. Another great feature with farming is compounding interest. You can choose to harvest from your farms (claim your LP tokens) and put them on another farm where they will compound and generate more income. Just like liquidity providers, yield farmers receive a share of rewards from the fees that traders pay to swap their tokens. yield farmers together with DEXs share commissions according to the proportion of their contribution in the liquidity pool as opposed to those fees going to centralized exchanges.

As with most good things, there are risks involved with being a liquidity provider or a yield farmer which include impermanent loss (IL). This happens when the price of one of the pairs in the liquidity pool drastically changes. For instance, if BTC grows steadily in price and your locked $2,500 would have made more money for you if it wasn't locked, but the price adjusts to balance your contribution. Impermanent loss is not that much of a big deal if you are on a great farm with good yields. The costly mistake that beginners make is that of chasing higher APY which happens on highly volatile markets. While APY may be high, this may also result in high IL due to volatility. The greater the price difference, the greater the IL. Sometimes you will realize that it would have been more worth it to hold your crypto instead of investing it. Which is why farming stablecoins is much safer; the APY is usually smaller on stable coins but it's consistent (Whiteboard Crypto, 2021c).

Choosing a Platform for Investment

There are several things to consider when choosing a platform to invest in, such as the number of assets available, the TVL, the APY, and the UI. With DeFi, you will see that you don't have to stick with one platform as there are no restrictions that exist with traditional institutions.

MakerDAO

MakerDAO is the first DeFi lending protocol that made DeFi what it is today. Built on the Ethereum blockchain, MakerDAO is a dual coin platform that amasses the highest TVLs of all lending protocols. With stablecoin DAI and governance token MAKR, users can lend, borrow, stake, and earn more from their crypto passively. MakerDAO offers one of the highest APY. Maker also has its own DEX, Oasis Trade (Andrei, 2021).

Compound Finance

One of the largest and trusted DeFi lending protocols, Compound Finance, allows users to instantly borrow or lend crypto from liquidity pools. Compound also has the governance token COMP, which grants users authority to vote on how the protocol is run and improved. Lenders get cTokens denoting their staked assets that they can use to get more assets to lock up in the protocol through leveraged borrowing (Wharton University of Pennsylvania, 2021).

Aave

The first lending protocol to offer flash loans, Aave was formerly known as ETHLend. The brainchild of *Stani Kulechov*, ETHLend hosted a successful ICO that brought in $16.2 million in 2017. It was through an announcement in the Bitcointalk forum that the rebranding to Aave was first mentioned in 2019. Holders of the previous coin LEND were able to migrate to the current native token AAVE with a 1:100 ratio. Holding AAVE has incentives and governance benefits for users. Aave lending protocol grants users a variety of over 20 digital assets including DAI and UNI (CoinGecko, n.d.-a).

CurveDAO

Having conducted one of the largest airdrops in 2020 to reward early users, Curve Finance is one of the most used AMM DEXs by yield farmers. With the focus to swap only tokens that have the same value, Curve offers protection from BTC and ETH crash by the opposite of impermanent loss as it buffs price volatility. It also introduced meta pools in order to promote liquidity of obscure tokens (CoinGecko, n.d.-b).

Risk and Challenges in Investment

Allow me to be transparent with you. Risk is everywhere, even where they claim risk-free! You saw that even banks are risky, and so is investing in the blockchain. While there are ways to mitigate risks, it is only wise to acknowledge its presence so that you are aware of it, and only then, will you actively opt for safety as you will not walk into things blindly just because they are hyped.

Investing in Something You Don't Understand

One of the biggest risks is ignorance. Not knowing the opportunities and risks that are associated with an entity is like walking into a dangerous place with your eyes closed. Blockchain is an enormous industry, without clear understanding, you can find yourself following the hype and riding a wave of excitement yet you don't know its driving force, until it deflates midway and you lose all that you put in it.

I'm glad that you have taken the first step to get informed, that already puts you ahead of those who have not discovered the potential and risks of investing in blockchain. I've pointed out on several occasions, and even put a disclaimer on this. Any information contained in this book is for educational purposes and to share my experience with you. It does not count as financial advice nor endorsement of projects reviewed here.

Scrutinize the information you find, seek proper financial advice from certified experts, follow your mentor's teachings, until you have a full understanding before parting with your money. Do not put your money in any of the mentioned protocols without due diligence, until your satisfaction. Do not invest in something that you don't understand, no matter how hyped it is.

Lack of Discipline

This is for either money or investment tools. Supposedly, you find that one of the projects covered here has potential to do a 10x or 1000x ROI—as most projects have done, anyway—while that might be true, do not ape-in without discipline. It's irresponsible to go all-in even if a project has great fundamentals. There are better ways to go about this, even if you can afford to lose your investment, ladder your purchases with discipline.

No Regulation

The fact that there is no government or authority calling people to order in the decentralized world means that malicious behavior usually goes unpunished.

Hacking

As you have already read under the insurance section, hacking is one of the highest risks that crypto platforms lose money. Hacking is like bank robbery. You don't always lose the money when hackers rob a platform that has been insured as that means your investment is covered. However, if hackers can steal more than an exchange is covered for, members will suffer a huge loss in the process. Even as an individual, you can be hacked. Besides insuring your crypto, you can opt to use cold storage which will not permanently protect you, but it will significantly reduce the risk.

Losing Your Wallet

It's possible to lose access to your wallet, by misplacing your private keys, or losing your seed phrases. Unlike with traditional and centralized finance where you can request assistance to reset your passwords if you've lost them, losing access to your crypto assets may be detrimental. Especially if you use non-custodial wallets, where it's your responsibility to safeguard your assets. Millions of bitcoin and other cryptocurrencies have been permanently lost (Royal, 2022).

Be careful with how you store your passwords. Always have a backup either on cloud storage for when you lose access to your devices, or offline in your safe.

Liquidation

This is especially true with trading and lending. This is when your position is closed at a loss to prevent blowing an account—including borrowed funds—by a CEX or DEX. Unfortunately, you cannot run away from being liquidated unless you don't trade or borrow anymore. However, you can minimize liquidation by trading a less lot size or having good asset management to trade a minimal percentage with less returns. Another way to avoid 100% liquidation is by using stop losses and take profit strategies, which are parameters that you set to indicate how much you're willing to risk.

Rug Pulls

As indicated with what made most ICOs to fail, project managers can abandon the project and run away with your money. You could become REKT (or utterly destroyed) if you join projects that are too good to be true. Always be safe and do your own research (DYOR).

Chapter 5: Exploring the DeFi Investment Portfolio

Invest in Coins and Future Blockchains

It is evident that blockchain technology is at its infancy with a potential to go mainstream. There are coins that you can grab while they are still affordable. Coins and blockchains that are directly or indirectly involved with Web 3.0 and the metaverse. The ways to choose a coin depends on a number of factors; utility being one of the core aspects to consider. There are over 12,000 coins listed on CoinMarketCap or CoinGecko, settling on which one to invest in really takes due diligence. Knowing what the coin is used for is essential to decide if it's plainly a meme, a clone, or something with tangible use cases as seen throughout this book. For instance, there are coins that are used by insurance protocols that have a growing blockchain offering low fees, and fast transactions; or simply put, coins that fall under the Layer 2 scaling solutions category. A coin with a good use case cements itself for a fruitful future. When its utility is rolled out, people will start to see its potential.

Blockchain-based coins also have greater potential to go parabolic depending on the type of blockchain and the consensus mechanism in place. These coins also have the native market, the users of that blockchain, which exposes them to an already existing fanbase. For example, SOL, AVAX, ADA, MATIC, and DOT, belong to ecosystems that have good fundamentals. Obtaining them at the dip, which has a wide gap from their ATH, could be an advantage. Other coins like MAKER, AAVE, and ALGO, are also great coins based one the global adoption of their underlying blockchains. Remember that I'm only expressing my views on projects that I think are solid, based on what we've already covered about them. This is not supposed to be taken as financial advice, or a sponsored recommendation about the projects. Be responsible for your own actions with your own money!

There is no denying that blockchain is still unfolding layer by layer. And there are trends that you need to follow if you want to remain liquid during all crypto seasons. When the bear season sets, the narrative is to hold more stablecoins, so that you'll be in a position to buy the dip, and so that you don't get frustrated watching your portfolio bleed throughout the entire bear market. Look for coins that have futuristic utility, like coins that are used in the metaverse, on NFT platforms, and those that are actively advocating for Web 3.0 implementation.

Having invested in coins that have great utility, like the ones mentioned in the paragraphs below, will give you confidence to HODL and approach your portfolio as a long-term investment. This is unless you have invested in seasonal meme coins, of which 90% of them are moonshots that strike and die; most get REKT anyway. So be wise when picking gems for the future, and if you approach this like a true crypto enthusiast, you already know that the market moves in seasons. There's a time to sow, and a time to reap. Remember, no matter how hyped a project is, always DYOR before *ape-ing*!

Privacy and Supply Chain Blockchains

Privacy

The main purpose behind the design of cryptos was to transact privately, hence the need to embed cryptography in currency. But most blockchains have neglected this in their process of providing other utility features. With some consensus mechanism protocols like proof-of-identity, the user even has to go as far as revealing their identity, by providing their KYC documents to prove their authenticity. Luckily, there are blockchains that have been true to the essence of privacy.

Crypton (CRP) and Utopia CRP Stablecoin (U USD)

Trusted and used as the main monetary unit by a large ecosystem, Utopia P2P, CRP boasts being one of the best privacy cryptos in circulation. Utopia P2P is an anonymous, multifaceted, and decentralized ecosystem that has functions such as messaging, mining, surfing, transacting, and data transmission. Created by The 1984 Group that stands for security and data privacy, this crypto provides transactions that are not recorded in the blockchain whatsoever. The ecosystem also has a stablecoin whose value is pegged to US dollar (U USD) (Matthew, 2021).

Monero (XMR)

Created as early as 2012, by the anonymous team of *Nicholas van Saberhagen*, Monero is one of the oldest, top-ranked privacy cryptocurrencies in the dark net. When law enforcement officers from different countries tried to censor usage of this coin, they could not even find details such as the number of transactions or number of users of this coin. Its mechanism uses complex cryptographic technologies such as Kovri, Stealth, and Ring CT to ensure the privacy of its users (Matthew, 2021).

Dash (DASH)

Also an early successor of Bitcoin, even dubbed an improved version of Bitcoin, Dash is one of the popular coins with a high level of security.

Verge (XVG)

Verge is also another crypto focused on the confidentiality of its users. It was launched in 2014 by a pseudonymous developer *Sunerok* (Matthew, 2021).

Komodo (KMD)

Forked from another privacy-based coin, ZCash, Komodo was invented by a pseudonymous crypto enthusiast, *jl777* in 2016, using delayed PoW (dPoW) consensus mechanism. Komodo also provides its users with complete anonymity and an additional tier of security (Matthew, 2021).

Supply Chain Blockchain

To improve agility, efficiency, and flexibility in supply chain companies, there is a rise in need of supply blockchains. Giant companies like IBM and Maersk, who collaborated to create TradersLens, an open and neutral supply chain platform reinforced by blockchain technology, are some of the first companies to merge crypto and supply chain. This brings industry innovation as well as reducing trade friction, and promoting global trade (GetSmarter, 2019).

In the supply chain, blockchain can help reduce food wastage by tracking food from farms to households, assist with quick settlements between retailers and suppliers, distribution of COVID-19 vaccines and relief funds (Coin Bureau, 2020).

VeChain (VET)

Using tamper-proof and distributed ledger technology, VeChain is one of the most popular supply-based cryptocurrencies. It was created in 2017 by the non-profit VeChain Foundation, manned by *Sunny Lu* (CoinGecko, n.d.-a) VeChain is one of the fastest growing projects that are partnering with a number of large entities. It was even honored as the best innovation in food supply for China in 2021 (Odunayo, 2021).

Waltonchain (WTC)

Waltonchain is regarded as a genuine, trustworthy, and traceable business ecosystem that is equipped with a team that is highly specialized in supply chain experience. It is mainly used to promote transparency, traceability, integrity, and monitoring of commodities in circulation. This blockchain combines blockchain with the internet of things (IoT), specifically the RFID—Waltonchain even gets its name from *Charlie Walton*, the inventor of RFID technology—technologies to create management systems for supply chains (CoinGecko, n.d.-b).

Hedera Hashgraph (HBAR)

A brainchild of *Dr Leemon Baird* and *Mance Harmon*, Hedera Hashgraph was funded through an ICO in August 2018, and was later launched in September 2019. Participants of the ICO and early investors were able to have access to the blockchain's native and utility token (HBAR) at the lowest price. HBAR powers Hedera services like smart contracts, file storage, and financial transactions. Hedera is now one of the most used, sustainable, enterprise-grade networks that allows businesses and individuals to operate efficiently in a decentralized economy (CoinMarketCap, n.d.-b). Hedera also partnered with an Australian food and wine tracing platform in 2020 (Haig, 2020).

The Market Analysis and Trading on Binance

There are ways in which you can predict market price action based on factors such as fundamental analysis, technical analysis, and intuitional analysis. One thing is clear, the market moves in cycles of highs and lows. In order to profit in trading, you need to know the instrument you're trading, fundamentals around it, and factors that influence its price action. You also need to know the right time frame and what different periods mean regarding that instrument in order for you to time your entries and exits. A market analysis is similar to a weather forecast; its indicators can give you a clear direction you have to take.

Fundamental Analysis

With any entity, determining whether it's a lucrative investment or not takes a look at its intrinsic value. This entails looking at the bigger picture of the tokenomics surrounding the project. Knowing the underlying information about a digital asset can help you evaluate whether it's overpriced or undervalued, and subsequently help you decide whether it's worth adding or removing from your long-term portfolio (Bybit Learn, 2021a).

Any tradable instrument whose value is not fixed can be affected by things like speeches,reports, management or structural changes, economic news, or any breaking news surrounding the project, or indirectly affecting it. Cryptocurrencies are no different, as they are subject to high volatility based on the above factors. Whether it's matured coins like Bitcoin and Ethereum, or new projects that recently joined the crypto space, cryptocurrencies are generally characterized with spiky movements, and therefore are associated with significant risks. It is paramount to know what is likely to be the main driving force that affects the price or determines the value of a crypto asset.

Today's Cryptocurrency Prices by Market Cap

The global crypto market cap is $1.53T, a 13.25% decrease over the last day. Read more

CoinMarketCap Predicts
Check Out the New Crypto Price Prediction Feature

Watchlist · Portfolio · Cryptocurrencies · Categories · DeFi · NFT · Polkadot Eco · BSC Eco · Solana Eco · Yield Farmi

#	Name	Price	24h %	7d %	Market Cap	Volume(24h)
1	Bitcoin BTC Buy	$36,450.39	8.86%	26.72%	$682,395,162,015	$80,172,454,425 2,198,614 BTC
2	Ethereum ETH Buy	$2,262.07	18.05%	44.26%	$262,474,326,820	$51,635,457,378 22,814,943 ETH
3	Tether USDT Buy	$1.00	0.07%	0.12%	$58,574,119,606	$171,612,489,745 171,430,183,618 USDT
4	Cardano ADA	$1.46	15.07%	31.38%	$46,609,592,184	$8,828,977,243 6,051,777,838 ADA
5	Binance Coin BNB Buy	$303.72	20.90%	49.48%	$46,622,424,935	$6,003,924,595 19,758,722 BNB
6	Dogecoin DOGE	$0.334	13.57%	36.59%	$43,437,828,514	$7,286,150,117 21,754,574,446 DOGE

Depending on whether you're looking at an asset as an investor or trader, two types of analysis are used. If you have an investor's cap on, you will look at things like the supply and demand of a project, the intended utility based on the problem it's designed to solve, as well as the team behind the project. Generally, cryptocurrencies have a hard cap, unlike fiat currency that can be reprinted as much as it needs to be. In the long run, the crypto with less supply is likely to grow more in value as that makes it deflationary.

Negative news like FUD are common to bring down the price of an asset. For instance, when China banned crypto mining, the price of Bitcoin and most altcoins crashed at the news. This was because China had the highest number of crypto miners due to the lower energy costs. This is a type of fundamental analysis. The markets took time to recover as miners were faced with closing shop or relocating, two decisions that need one to have a clear mind (Watcher Guru, 2021).

When the Federal Reserve hinted at increasing interest rates, the news had a negative effect on the crypto markets, and pretty much, whenever *Jerome Powell* coughs, the markets, whether stocks, indices, and crypto, catch the flu (R, 2021). FUD needs an investor who is aware of them so that they take calculated risks. Take advantage by buying the dip, or by getting out of projects that face serious structural change, and wait for another opportunity to board the ship again.

At the time of writing this part, there's FUD around the Fantom network, because *Andrea Conje*, one of the key developers on the project, just announced that he's taking a break from crypto. As you would have guessed, Fantom token FTM took a major dip to $1.43 (Crypto Banter, 2022). This news brings FUD to investors, as day traders are taking advantage to scalp FTM, and investors with paper hands end up selling, not looking at the bigger picture. However, this a decentralized network, and Conje leaving the project, doesn't necessarily mean it's the end of it; in fact, traders are already eating the dip. But this fundamental analysis is bound to affect the performance of FTM, as it already has, maybe it will even take time to recover, based on how the remaining team decides to regain the trust of their community.

Some of the factors to consider that contribute to the fundamental analysis include the project status in terms of active addresses or the community at large, change in consensus, or any improvement in the tokenomics. A project that has an increasing number of active users somehow promises a bullish future. While a project that has few addresses holding a large capacity of coins indicates the unsafety of that particular project, as this means that any of these addresses that got in early, whenever they reach their desired milestone, they may sell-off and cause the asset to decline massively.

With regards to improvement in consensus, this means that the project that was using PoW, which has its shortcomings like the large carbon footprint, block traffic, and high fees, is now exploring an alternative consensus that will improve its scalability, reduce block congestion, reduce transaction fees, while also choosing to be environmentally-friendly. An example of this is with the long-anticipated Ethereum 2.0, which claims its transition from PoW to PoS. This positive news on Ethereum contributes to good fundamentals on the network and related blockchains, and thus, may mean that Ethereum is a good long-term project to hold.

The hash rate of the project is also a good tool to determine the fundamentals surrounding it. Typically, investors find hash rates as a good-health indicator for the blockchain, and thus, use them to determine the future of the project (Bybit Learn, 2021a).

Technical Analysis

Technical analysis is using indicators, price action, price charts, and trendlines to analyze the possible direction of the market. Trading using technical analysis is studying historical data and using it to predict the future performance. That is because the market in most cases moves in a repetitive cycle. The price is either high or low, and even if it doesn't return to the same price, it moves in such a way that it allows opportunities to buy when the price has dropped and to sell when the price has gone up.

Support and Resistance Zones

The market has periods where prices are moving in a declining or ascending trend. There are areas where the price of an asset reaches more than once before it breaks that level. In an uptrend, the level where the market peaks and reverses before it rises to reach that peak again, is called resistance. The price can reach resistance levels a number of times, struggling to break through. Resistance acts as a ceiling of the price, that the asset can't seem to surpass.

The opposite is true for a descending market whereby the price drops to a certain level and bounces. The lowest price that the market reaches in a downtrend which acts as the floor is called support. Similarly, the price has to hit the support zone several times before it qualifies as an official pivotal point. It is important to note that support and resistance can occur several times in different zones, with the time frame as a distinguishing factor. You can have support levels on a shorter time frame and when you zoom out for a bird's-eye view it indicates that it was just a mini-support within a larger resistance zone.

Another important aspect to note is that support and resistance are not lines, but zones. This means that you can have a range of variables within a zone that the price can reverse at, or identify as support or resistance areas. When you set your trading parameters such as stop losses or take profits, put this in mind and don't look to set them on the exact lines but always leave room for deviation within a certain range.

Chart Patterns

Technical analysis also includes studying charts to look for clues. Traders know that the market always leaves clues. Some assets move in predictable patterns according to their seasons. During the bear season, that is basically categorized with more people selling their assets and the markets subsequently declining in value. Traders make money by following the trend and going short (selling), with the anticipation that the price will reach an oversold area, where bears lose the power to the bulls. Just like with fundamental analysis, the strength of supply and demand can be seen by studying the chart patterns, candlestick formations, and technical indicators like relative strength iIndex (RSI).

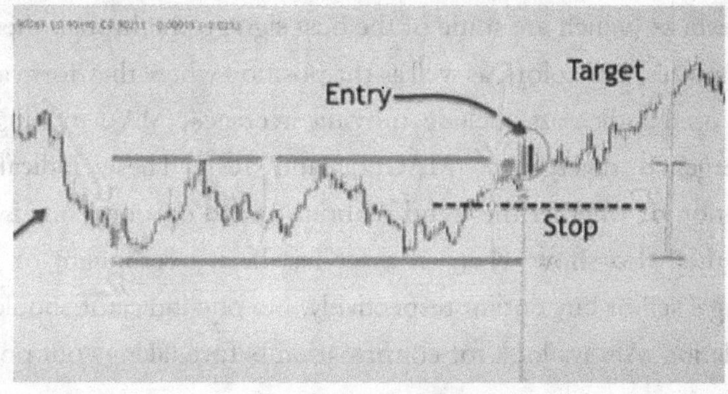

Most known chart patterns include the ascending triangle pattern which appears in an uptrend and categorized by an ascending support line with resistance in a horizontal line. When this pattern occurs, normally the market breaks in a continuous uptrend. The opposite is true for a descending triangle that usually means the market will break downwards. Other patterns take the form of an asymmetric triangle, double bottom, double top, head and shoulders, and kettle and cup. Since this is not much of a technical trading analysis guide, I'll not go in-depth with these patterns.

In order to read the charts well, traders can either study candlestick patterns which show the opening, closing, highest and lowest prices. And as with the charts patterns and support and resistance above, the longer time frames give a clear indication of the trend. Profitable traders know that the trend should be your friend, meaning that you should trade in the direction of the trend rather than trading the opposite. In an uptrend, look for higher lows to use as entry points and put your take profits or exit at higher highs. And in a downward trend, look for lower highs to take your sell positions and use the lower lows to take your profits.

Technical Indicators

There are numerous technical analysis indicators used in most CEXs or any trading-equipped platforms. In addition to using chart patterns and candlesticks (which are some of the best sign givers through their varying shapes, sizes, and colors, as well as the position where they form a pattern), most used indicators include moving averages (MA), moving average convergence divergence (MACD), and RSI. These indicators give indication of whether the trend is about to end or a new one is about to start, they also show when an asset has been overbought or oversold, hinting a sell or buy option respectively. No one indicator should be used in isolation. Always look for confirmation before taking your position.

Types of Trading

Arbitrage

As you already saw throughout the document, arbitrage trading is one of the most common types in the DeFi landscape. This type of trading involves buying a certain asset from one exchange and selling it almost instantly on another exchange. It is one of the reasons why traders take out flash loans from the lending protocols, knowing that they will refund the DEX after a series of steps that usually happen in one smart contract transaction. Due to the use of AMMs, it is common to find market prices slightly different across exchanges. So you can borrow a stablecoin and use it to purchase a volatile asset from an exchange where it's listed cheaper, and sell it to the DEX where it is selling higher, and profit from the price discrepancies. Arbitrage trading exists even on CEXs like Binance, where you can buy and sell assets with deviating prices without the need to acquire a flash loan.

Futures

Futures trading involves taking a contract to buy or sell an asset at a date set in future. As previously mentioned, futures trading involves taking a leveraged position by borrowing funds from an exchange. This type of trading is usually used to hedge, scalp, or to make quick money by moving against the contracted position to make profits along the way to the intended event. This is so that even if the buyer loses on that trade, they would've taken advantage with leveraged trades prior to expiry of the contract. Futures is a growing trend in DeFi, but it's not new on CEXs. While it has potential to make massive profits, any spiky movement against your scalping positions can have your trades closed on a huge minus (liquidation).

Margin or Leveraged Trading

Binance and other CEXs are preferred by traders for trading margins and taking leveraged positions. Similar to futures trading, traders can make massive profits within a short period of time because they are allowed with more money than they have. When the market takes sharp dives or spikes against their traded positions, they receive a margin call, which is a notification to add more funds or to have their positions closed on a loss so that the exchange gets its funds that the trader leveraged with. In most cases, traders even lose their collateral, or their initial deposits. Both margin and futures trading should not be explored without a mentor and frugal training. With tools like stop loss, trail stop, and take profit, traders can protect their accounts from huge losses.

Options Trading

Trading options is one of the easiest forms of trading as it entails predicting the direction of the upcoming market movement within a specified period. Unlike with options above, this type charges the trader the cost of that trade upon execution, leaving the option to lose it if the market goes against their traded direction or to have it refunded with profit in the event that their prediction is correct. There are only two trading options: Call when you predict a price increase and put if you think the price will fall. It is another growing niche in both CEXs and DEXs.

Spot Trading

It is probably one of the safest types of trading. As the name indicates, spot trading entails buying or selling an asset with the current price on the spot. The price that you see, is what you pay or earn if you're selling. Spot trading is best used with the hold on for dear life (HODL) strategy, whereby you do proper fundamental analysis of a project and buy it on the spot to hold on for dear life because you believe that it will grow in value. The simplest way to succeed in spot trading is to always buy low and sell high, or as traders say, "buy the dip and sell the top". As we already specified that the market moves in cycles and that the trend should be your friend, if the price is too high, you can wait for the dip to buy an asset. That's if it will because with some assets, once they go parabolic, you can only wish that they will give you an entry opportunity as they usually don't. That said, spot trading still needs to be treated with discipline.

Cut Down Taxes for DeFi

The issue of taxes on cryptos is still the biggest elephant in the room. While the infrastructure bill that the president of the United States, Joe Biden, signed in 2021 suggests that crypto brokers must report their users when they make capital gains. Major exchanges like Coinbase, Kraken, and FTX spent around $2.2 million in lobbying activities, seeking further clarification on what this entails. The bill has already been signed to take effect in January 2024, stating that anyone facilitating a serial crypto exchange is regarded as a broker, and that the exchanges must report anyone transacting (receiving) with $10,000 worth of stablecoins and above must provide evidence within 15 days on the source of funds and other private information to avoid being charged with a felony (Constantino, 2021).

Initially, crypto exchanges were not liable to reporting any gains or losses to the internal revenue service (IRS). This somehow gave taxpayers a trump card of not fully disclosing their crypto capital gains or income, therefore, cheating the system (Hsieh, 2021). But since the bill has been passed, crypto exchanges are forced to start reporting to the IRS and their customers effective in 2023, to be added in the tax reports for 2024. You must bear in mind that CEXs basically collect personal data of their users to comply with KYC regulations and anti-money laundering policies. This means that they have your information, and to avoid being fined, they will likely comply with the regulation.

As for DEXs, which do not really have personal details of their users, there might be a long way to go before they're forced to report any sort of data. This is especially because most traders buy an asset on one platform, and sell it on another, making it difficult for DEXs to report if there has been any capital gains. It poses a problem of whether the trader must pay taxes twice with data recorded across different exchanges or only when they exchange crypto for fiat. But you personally, do have to report on capital gains and income realized through DeFi platforms to avoid any audits that may get you in trouble.

Some Tax Hacks to Consider

Consult a Qualified Tax Advisor

The best hack is to probably get a professional if you don't know what you're doing, or you're having challenges with figuring out how to compile your tax report. That's because you don't want to find yourself making a costly mistake that can get you punished for tax evasion. However, with a professional, you can work out strategies on how to avoid or minimize taxes on your crypto gains.

Use a Crypto Tax Calculator

If you know how to navigate through your platforms, you can use portfolio trackers and import your activities to a crypto tax calculator. A crypto tax calculating software like Koinly is free to use and is compatible with most large exchanges like Binance and Coinbase. Other well-known crypto tax softwares include Cointracker which automatically generates tax calculations based on your portfolio using five different tax form methods: Highest in, first out (HIFO); first in, first out (FIFO); last in, first out (LIFO); adjusted cost base (ACB); and share pooling. Cointracker is also integrated with TurboTax. Blox, Blockpit, BearTax, and CryptoTaxCalculator.io also make it to the list of widely used tax softwares that support a variety of crypto assets across multiple exchanges. In any case, getting a tax professional might be your best bet if you're not familiar with compiling tax reports (Gupta, 2021).

Set-Up a Charity

As you may know, charities don't pay taxes. And there are tax benefits for you when you donate money to a charity. This will only work if you have not sold your crypto and generally have long-term gains that could result in taxes ranging from 5%–25% depending on your state. With your lawyer, you can set up a Charitable Remainder Trust (CRT) fund where you will donate your crypto gains to.

That would mean identifying a legitimate 501(c)(3) charity, and nominating yourself as a lifetime beneficiary of that CRT. Once a CRT is set up, you can donate a big chunk of your crypto to its separate crypto wallet, which will instantly give you tax deductions for donating money to your own charity. Because you are not donating directly to that 501(c)(3)

charity until you die, you do not get 100% tax deduction, but over a period of five years you get up to 60% deduction (Maher, 2021).

Your CRT can then sell the crypto and buy more crypto or other assets. Then you can set up an annuity plan for it, which will be paid to you as the beneficiary until you die, bearing in mind that annuities are taxed at a regular income tax scale. That's where you can use that tax deduction benefit of five years. This will save you a lot of money and benefit society in the process. So how does this benefit your own beneficiaries? Does all the money go to charity? Not quite. You can set up an irrevocable life insurance trust (ILIT) to take out insurance policy cover on yourself that you will pay from your annuity income, which you can pay off in advance during the five years of tax benefits, or little by little, if you prefer. At the end, from your crypto profit, a charity will benefit from your donated funds (and its gains), you will receive tax exemptions, annual income, and your family will be taken care of, should your time run out (Maher, 2021).

Register a Home-Based Business

Whether you're a full-time crypto trader or just a HODLer, you can take advantage of registering a home-based business as this will allow certain purchases to count as business expenses instead of luxuries. For instance, to get that yacht you've always wanted, you can buy it but list it as a living expense for your business if you conduct your business from it. Or that luxury trip to Bali. You can couple it with a few business meetings (with fine dining) and list it as a business expense. That is how the rich avoid taxes.

Buy Crypto in Your IRA

Another way you can avoid paying taxes is by buying crypto as part of your retirement plan. If you buy it within your traditional individual retirement account (IRA), you'll be exempted from paying taxes until you take your distributions. However, if you buy within a tax-advantaged individual account like ROTH IRA, you will pay zero taxes on the capital gains in that account. For more stringent measures to totally avoid taxes on your crypto, you can open an offshore, limited liability company (LLC) IRA and move your funds. In this manner, you will be the full custodian of your crypto. You can even use your IRA to find residency in countries like Panama and Nicaragua (Staffwriter, 2022).

Wash Sale

Wash sale is the act of selling a security at a loss and almost immediately buying back the same security, or asset, or a substantially identical asset within 30 days before or after sale. The IRS prohibits this wash sale for securities like stocks and indices, but in their 2014 article, cryptos are listed as property, and thus, exempt from this rule. This means that you can sell your crypto when you're at a loss from the time you bought it, in order to register that capital loss for tax benefits, and immediately buy it back within 30 days because this wash sale is allowed with cryptos. This regulation is an old one but the IRS article has not yet changed this yet, so that is a hack you can still make use of, for now (Chandrasekera, 2020).

Crypto Gifting

Receiving a gift in the form of crypto, cashing it out, and spending it is not taxable. Therefore, you can use this strategy with the people whom you trust to give them cryptos as gifts to buy items that you will personally use even though they are registered in their names. Of course, this will only work with people whom you completely trust that they won't hesitate to handover your 'gifts'.

Hype of NFTs and the Future

Decentralization opened the whole new world, starting with the way we handle money to expanding into the art industry, and finding a stance in almost every business landscape. Amidst the DeFi craze, a sub-niche evolved and took the world by storm through NFTs. These are unique tokens that have unfixed value which is dependent on the demand, team behind, use case, and rarity of a project. One of the key features of NFTs is their scarcity, which is deflationary. For instance, there are only 10,000 unique Bored Apes, and with most celebrities flaunting them on their social media pages, their demand is too high and hence their price is equally high (Pastel, 2022).

It's important to note that NFTs precede DeFi, although they recently gained traction in an overlapping timeline, highlighting even more use cases of DeFi and the blockchain. Some of the first NFTs date as far back as 2014 while DeFi was coined in 2017 (Di Liscia, 2021). Similar to DeFi, NFTs still receive criticism that they are over-hyped and that their bubble will burst when their lack of intrinsic value is realized, but the charts tell a different story as the total value locked in NFTs increases, and they are well-received.

When the NFT trend began to gain popularity between 2019 and 2021, it's highly possible that no one envisioned millions of dollars worth of NFTs. As it stands, the most expensive NFT at the moment is the $91.8 million worth of NFT mass, called *The Merge* by a cryptic digital artist, *Pak*

(Cryptory, 2022). Pak broke *Mike Winkelmann's* record for the most expensive NFT sold for Winkelmann's work, *The Everydays: The First 5000 Days* in December 2021. The Everydays remain one of the most famous and acknowledged works of art in the NFT landscape, with Winkelmann, or Beeple as he's known in the crypto art space, recently expanding his work into artwork for walls as he launched a collaboration with *Jack Hanley Gallery* (Small, 2022).

NFTs have not only disrupted traditional art—as evidenced by the attacks that suggest NFT art is not art—but this branch of decentralization seems to be going mainstream in more ways than one. Looking at NFT use cases, which are taking blockchain uses to a whole new level, the future of decentralization is no longer a far-fetched anticipated theory but history in the making. For the same reasons of tracking the history, verifying provenance, and giving total ownership over the content by the creators, NFTs resemble DeFi and improve on the shortcomings of centralized authorities.

Some of the remarkable use cases of NFTs include inspiring charitable donations, ownership of sporting events highlights, provable artwork, supply chain, and in the entertainment industry through content that creators own and have the ability to sell directly to their fans without intermediaries. They would also have the ability to receive recurring royalties as fans resell the work and profit from it. The gaming experiences and investment opportunities with in-gaming items that are sold as NFTs are also the reason behind the exponential growth of this industry.

NFTs began with art, but their deployment in different sectors show echoes of the desired ability for technologies to work in sync, be interoperable, and have composable synergy. Allow me to make a bold statement, that we have not seen anything yet as far as this industry is concerned. That means, we ought to be more prepared for the future, and where we can become early adopters to the technology, let's lead the way.

The anticipated metaverse awaits to be explored rather than criticized, so let's take lead in exploring what the decentralized future entails for us. This book is my way of throwing you a life line. It's up to you whether you grab it and hold on tightly, and I hope you embrace it.

Conclusion

The potential of DeFi to dominate the financial landscape continues to grow exponentially! While it is clear that DeFi is still in its developmental stage, the rate at which the emerging protocols, services, and categories within it have more wealth flowing towards, is enough evidence that DeFi will be the wealth destination. Otherwise, we would not be seeing traditional houses seeking their piece of the pie in trying to incorporate stability of fixed assets like fiat currency with the digitization of money through CBDCs.

Congratulations for taking this journey with me to this honeyed end where you are one book wiser. I hope that you found the expansive content, though probably over-simplified for veterans, useful and applicable in your own decentralized financial expedition. The aim was to bring balanced material that accommodates late DeFi adopters and seasoned crypto enthusiasts, to point you at trends that you may be familiar with, so that you have a confirmation on how diverse this niche is. It's also to show how you can leverage on different protocols and services to mitigate your risks and have a more diversified portfolio.

I believe that Web 3.0, NFTs, and the future of DeFi are no longer a mystery to you. I also hope that the covered material will act as a compass to direct your next move, should you have a specific sub-topic that you want to dive deeper in. *Mastering Decentralized Finance (DeFi)* was written with you in mind, to echo on the importance of interoperable networks and multifaceted protocols, and to give you exposure to the benefits of decentralization as a whole, as well as to mark this pivotal point towards mass adoption of DeFi.

If blockchain was ever a complicated concept for you, I hope that I was able to decouple it to your liking. I've given you an overview of DeFi services, and why I think it's the future that we should rather be prepared to bask in than fight it. A friendly reminder is that there are risks in every financial model, so you need to make the safety of your funds a priority. Just as this niche is fascinating to us with the good will, it is worth noting that it is also becoming a thrill sport for sophisticated hackers. Treat every shared tip in this book with caution, that way, you'll be exercising authority and responsibility over your own funds. It's my wish that you stay in the decentralized world for the longest time to have your own success stories from being cautious, attentive to detail, and adventurous enough to take calculated risks. The future is risky anyway! You might as well start now to be comfortable with risk.

I truly hope that you found value through this guide, and if you did, I'll appreciate you leaving a positive review so that others can be exposed to this material as well. Thank you, once more, for journeying with me throughout this book.

Hey Friends!

How has been your experience after reading the book?

Hope that this book improves your life, health and wellbeing. Your precious feedback would be of great value for us and help us improve.

Thanks and Stay Connected with us for FREE Goodies at:

info@hafizpublications.com
Visit us at : hafizpublications.com

References

Adams, H. (2019, February 11). *A short history of Uniswap*. Uniswap Protocol. https://uniswap.org/blog/uniswap-history

Aki, J. (2020, January 30). *What are decentralized exchanges and why should you try them?* BeInCrypto. https://beincrypto.com/learn/decentralized-exchanges/

Alexandria. (n.d.). *Throughput | CoinMarketCap*. CoinMarketCap Alexandria. Retrieved February 19, 2022, from https://coinmarketcap.com/alexandria/glossary/throughput

Andrei, V. (2021, March 24). *DeFi lending: Aave vs. Maker vs. Compound*. Albaron Ventures. https://albaronventures.com/defi-lending-aave-vs-maker-vs-compound/

Arti. (2021, October 24). *Top 10 best cryptocurrency DEX aggregators in 2021*. Analytics Insight. https://www.analyticsinsight.net/top-10-best-cryptocurrency-dex-aggregators-in-2021/

BarnBridge. (2021, August 27). *What is BarnBridge?* [Video]. YouTube. https://www.youtube.com/watch?v=aqC_r7SPX-g&t=2s

Belford, C. (2021). *Cryptocurrency DeFI guidebook: A beginner to expert guide on decentralized finance: DeFi and blockchain, borrow, lend, trade, save & invest after Bitcoin & Ethereum in peer to peer lending & farming* (pp. 116–118). Silk Publishing. https://www.goodreads.com/book/show/58985480-cryptocurrency-defi-guidebook

Bhattacharya, J. (2021, December 20). *What is Web 3.0? The future of the internet*. Single Grain. https://www.singlegrain.com/web3/web-3-0/

Bigelow, S. J. (2021). *What is edge computing? Everything you need to know*. SearchDataCenter. https://www.techtarget.com/searchdatacenter/definition/edge-computing

BitBoy Crypto. (2022, January 3). *Top Defi platforms for 2022 (200% crypto gains for max profit)* [Video]. YouTube. https://www.youtube.com/watch?v=A-00X2YSnIg0

Boyan, A. (2020, March 10). *What's with DeFi and money legos?* Our Status. https://our.status.im/whats-with-defi-and-money-legos/

Bybit Learn. (2021a, June 16). *How to analyze a cryptocurrency using fundamental analysis.* https://learn.bybit.com/investing/how-to-analyze-a-cryptocurrency-using-fundamental-analysis/

Bybit Learn. (2021b, October 20). *What is an initial exchange offering (ICO) in crypto?* https://learn.bybit.com/crypto/what-are-initial-exchange-offerings-ieos/

Bybit Learn. (2021c, November 19). *What is perpetual protocol (PERP)? A beginner's guide.* https://learn.bybit.com/altcoins/perp/

Campbell, L. (n.d.). *DeFi wallets - Best crypto wallets for decentralized finance.* DeFi Rate. https://defirate.com/wallet/

Campbell, L. (2022). *Argent wallet review - Argent crypto smart wallet.* DeFi Rate. https://defirate.com/argent/

Carr, N., & Zhou, G. C. (2021, October 27). *De-Fi lending: Flash loans – Fintech Research Lab.* The University of Texas at Austin. https://sites.utexas.edu/fintechresearchlab/2021/10/27/de-fi-lending-flash-loans-in-depth/

Chainwire. (2022, January 18). *AutoSwap brings limit orders and stop losses to Trader Joe and Avalanche, powered by Autonomy Network.* Securities.io. https://www.securities.io/autoswap-brings-limit-orders-and-stop-losses-to-trader-joe-and-avalanche-powered-by-autonomy-network/

Chan, D. (2022, January 26). *OKX review 2022 | Fees, facts & warnings.* Marketplace Fairness. https://www.marketplacefairness.org/cryptocurrency/okx-review/

Chandrasekera, S. (2020, February 19). *A tax loophole every crypto trader should know.* Forbes. https://www.forbes.com/sites/shehanchandrasekera/2020/02/19/

a-tax-loophole-every-crypto-trader-should-know/?sh=6809e027ddfc

Che, C. (2021, October 27). *DeFi: Can decentralized finance defy China's crypto controls?* SupChina. https://supchina.com/2021/10/27/defi-can-decentralized-finance-defy-chinas-crypto-controls/

Chen, H. S., Jarrell, J. T., Carpenter, K. A., Cohen, D. S., & Huang, X. (2019). Blockchain in healthcare: A patient-centered model. *Biomedical Journal of Scientific & Technical Research*, *20*(3), 15017–15022. https://www.ncbi.nlm.nih.gov/pmc/articles/PMC6764776/

Clark, M. (2022, January 18). *Coinbase NFT marketplace partners Mastercard.* Blockchain Reporter. https://blockchainreporter.net/coinbase-nft-marketplace-partners-mastercard/

Coin Bureau. (2020, November 22). *Supply chain blockchains: Set to explode in 2021?* [Video]. YouTube. https://www.youtube.com/watch?v=2RFxO52Go0M

Coin Bureau. (2021, February 27). *Uniswap or Pancakeswap: Battle of the DEXs!!* [Video]. YouTube. https://www.youtube.com/watch?v=7rEqGX4eRnk

CoinDesk. (2021, July 24). *The demise of "OpenBazaar" and Web 3.0's future* [Video]. YouTube. https://www.youtube.com/watch?v=ck6e5dKZ3h4

CoinFox. (2015, August 20). *The father of smart contracts compared the decision on block size with the Shuttle Challenger disaster*. Coinfox. https://www.coinfox.info/news/2805-the-father-of-smart-contracts-compared-the-decision-on-block-size-with-the-shuttle-challenger-disaster

CoinGecko. (n.d.-a). *Aave price today, chart, and market cap.* https://www.coingecko.com/en/coins/aave

CoinGecko. (n.d.-b). *Curve DAO token price, CRV chart, and market cap.* https://www.coingecko.com/en/coins/curve-dao-token

CoinGecko. (n.d.-c). *VeChain price, VET chart, and market cap.* https://www.coingecko.com/en/coins/vechain

CoinGecko. (n.d.-d). *Waltonchain price, WTC chart, and market cap.* https://www.coingecko.com/en/coins/waltonchain

CoinGecko. (2022a, March 11). *Uniswap price, UNI chart, and market cap.* https://www.coingecko.com/en/coins/uniswap

CoinGecko. (2022b, March 12). *Cryptocurrency global charts.* https://www.coingecko.com/en/global_charts

Coingecko. (2022, February 21). *USD Coin price, USDC chart, and market cap.* CoinGecko. https://www.coingecko.com/en/coins/usd-coin

CoinGenius. (2020, July 1). *DeFi Asset Management* [Video]. YouTube. https://www.youtube.com/watch?v=EB9SqIRtFu8

CoinMarketCap. (n.d.-a). *dYdX price today, DYDX to USD live, market cap and chart.* https://coinmarketcap.com/currencies/dydx/

CoinMarketCap. (n.d.-b). *Hedera price today, HBAR to USD live, market cap and chart.* https://coinmarketcap.com/currencies/hedera/

CoinMarketCap. (2021, December 20). *What's Web 3.0? [All your questions answered]* [Video]. YouTube. https://www.youtube.com/watch?v=yLPfPqbAlJw

Coinsider. (2018, September 21). *Proof of what?! Overview of 13 different consensus algorithms for cryptocurrencies!* [Video]. YouTube. https://www.youtube.com/watch?v=ah94PuwR1DI&t=26s

CoinTelegraph. (2021, June 10). *Yieldly debuts DeFi on Algorand with $8M TVL in first 48 hours.* https://cointelegraph.com/press-releases/yieldly-debuts-defi-on-algorand-with-8m-tvl-in-first-48-hours

Comben, C. (2019, June 4). *How does the proof of authority algorithm work?* Yahoo. https://finance.yahoo.com/news/does-proof-authority-algorithm-090006261.html

Constantino, T. (2021, November 5). *NYU public policy professor gives crypto industry a solid "B" grade for recent lobbying activities.* The Motley Fool. https://www.fool.com/the-ascent/cryptocurrency/articles/nyu-public-policy-professor-gives-crypto-industry-a-solid-b-grade-for-recent-lobbying-activities/

Corporate Finance Institute. (n.d.). *Smart contracts - Overview, uses, benefits, limitations.* https://corporatefinanceinstitute.com/resources/knowledge/deals/smart-contracts/

Crunchbase. (n.d.). *Opyn - Crunchbase company profile & funding.* Crunchbase. https://www.crunchbase.com/organization/opyn

Crypto Banter. (2022, March 6). *Is this the end of Fantom? | Andre Cronje quits crypto* [Video]. YouTube. https://www.youtube.com/watch?v=i_yjNDJbAK4

Crypto Corner. (2019, August 30). *Genesis block, block size, block height, block time, block reward, block timestamp explained* [Video]. YouTube. https://www.youtube.com/watch?v=SBaqGKyjFBA

Crypto Gems. (2021, June 4). *IEO vs IDO explained | What happened in 2017 ICO explosion?* [Video]. YouTube. https://www.youtube.com/watch?v=e2OgpfvpaA8

Cryptopedia Staff. (2021a, March 15). *What is an automated market maker (AMM)?* Gemini. https://www.gemini.com/cryptopedia/amm-what-are-automated-market-makers

Cryptopedia Staff. (2021b, November 30). *Hegic: ERC-20 token for crypto options trading.* Gemini. https://www.gemini.com/cryptopedia/hegic-hegic-defi-options-trading-protocol-on-ethereum#section-hegic-platform-structure-and-liquidity-pools

CryptoRobin News. (2021, July 22). *BarnBridge ($BOND) - A DeFi protocol for tokenizing risk | Review | CryptoRobin* [Video]. YouTube. https://www.youtube.com/watch?v=LMP1_59sT_s

Cryptory. (2022, January 6). *The Merge – The most expensive NFT in the world.* https://en.cryptory.net/post/the-merge-the-most-expensive-nft-in-the-world/

Daly, L. (2021, October 12). *What is an initial coin offering (ICO)?* The Motley Fool. https://www.fool.com/investing/stock-market/market-sectors/financials/cryptocurrency-stocks/initial-coin-offering/

Dana, E. (2022, February 7). *BarnBridge partners with optimism to launch SMART Alpha pools for Synthetix and Chainlink*. Medium. https://medium.com/barnbridge/barnbridge-partners-with-optimism-to-launch-smart-alpha-pools-for-synthetix-and-chainlink-388bd207802e

Daryanani, L. (2021, October 2). *Aave, Maker, Compound: This is the right way to gauge their value*. AMBCrypto. https://ambcrypto.com/aave-maker-compound-this-is-the-right-way-to-gauge-their-value/

Defi Donut. (2021, December 7). *Pool together: 30 days results | Getting paid to save* [Video]. YouTube. https://www.youtube.com/watch?v=Xpqtm4NgZlw

Di Liscia, V. (2021, June 10). *"First ever NFT" sells for $1.4 million*. Hyperallergic. https://hyperallergic.com/652671/kevin-mccoy-quantum-first-nft-created-sells-at-sothebys-for-over-one-million/

Dickens, S. (2021, December 31). *The five biggest cryptocurrency hacks of the year*. Yahoo. https://finance.yahoo.com/news/five-biggest-cryptocurrency-hacks-110016976.html

Duke University. (n.d.). *Misunderstandings - DeFi myths and facts*. Coursera. https://www.coursera.org/lecture/decentralized-finance-infrastructure-duke/misunderstandings-mmacs

Dutta, R. (2021, November 30). *Advancing DeFi lending with a social graph credit system*. Nasdaq.com. https://www.nasdaq.com/articles/advancing-defi-lending-with-a-social-graph-credit-system

Editorial Team. (2021, April 23). *Kucoin review 2021: Safe crypto exchange? | Everything we found out*. Coin Bureau. https://www.coinbureau.com/review/kucoin-exchange/

Ethereum. (2014, July 29). *Vitalik Buterin explains Ethereum* [Video]. YouTube. https://www.youtube.com/watch?v=TDGq4aeevgY

Ethereum.org. (n.d.). *What is Ethereum?* https://ethereum.org/en/what-is-ethereum/

Ethos. (2018, April 5). *What is Ethereum gas? Ethereum gas explained* [Video]. YouTube. https://www.youtube.com/watch?v=AJvzNICwcwc

Faridi, O. (2021, June 7). *Oliver Xie: Founder at DeFi insurance protocol InsurAce explains how platform addresses risks from smart contract vulnerabilities*. Crowdfund Insider. https://www.crowdfundinsider.com/2021/06/175920-oliver-xie-founder-at-defi-insurance-protocol-insurace-explains-how-platform-addresses-risks-from-smart-contract-vulnerabilities/

Finematics. (2021a, January 30). *Derivatives in DEFI explained (Synthetix, UMA, Hegic, Opyn, Perpetual, dYdX, BarnBridge)* [Video]. YouTube. https://www.youtube.com/watch?v=QxoqPZRw9y4

Finematics. (2021b, June 24). *Bank run in DEFI - Lessons learned from the Iron Finance collapse* [Video]. YouTube. https://www.youtube.com/watch?v=HUokre-szPg

Foxley, W. (2019, November 15). *German regulator orders "KaratGold Coin" issuer to cease operations*. CoinDesk. https://www.coindesk.com/markets/2019/11/15/german-regulator-orders-karatgold-coin-issuer-to-cease-operations/

Frankenfield, J. (2021a, July 20). *DigiCash*. Investopedia. https://www.investopedia.com/terms/d/digicash.asp

Frankenfield, J. (2021b, November 30). *Consensus mechanism (Cryptocurrency)*. Investopedia. https://www.investopedia.com/terms/c/consensus-mechanism-cryptocurrency.asp

Freiberg, L. (2020, October 19). *Empty Set Dollar (ESD)*. Medium. https://medium.com/@lewisfreiberg/empty-set-dollar-esd-a0abbfc5ecdb

Ganti, A. (2021, December 26). *What is asset management?* Investopedia. https://www.investopedia.com/terms/a/assetmanagement.asp

Gauba, A. (2021, June 16). *Opyn v2 FAQ*. GitHub. https://github.com/opynfinance/v2-documentation/blob/main/getting-started/introduction.md

GetSmarter. (2019, January 21). *How blockchain will radically improve the supply chain*. https://www.getsmarter.com/blog/market-trends/how-blockchain-will-radically-improve-the-supply-chain/

Gupta, A. (2021). *9 best cryptocurrency tax calculator for filling crypto tax 2021» CoinFunda*. CoinFunda. https://coinfunda.com/cryptocurrency-tax-calculator-apps/

Haig, S. (2020, September 22). *South Australian food and wine tracing platform teams up with Hedera*. Cointelegraph. https://cointelegraph.com/news/south-australian-food-and-wine-tracing-platform-teams-up-with-hedera

Hamilton, D. (2021, March 7). *Investing in PancakeSwap (CAKE) – Everything you need to know*. Securities.io. https://www.securities.io/investing-in-pancakeswap-cake-everything-you-need-to-know/

Harshman, J. (2022, January 14). *The 10 best crypto coins to stake*. CreditDonkey. https://www.creditdonkey.com/best-coins-to-stake.html

Harvard University. (2021). *Encode AMA series: Hugh Karp, founder of Nexus Mutual*. https://rcc.harvard.edu/event/encode-ama-series-hugh-karp-founder-nexus-mutual

Hayes, A. (2019, June 25). *What ever happened to the dotcom bubble?* Investopedia. https://www.investopedia.com/terms/d/dotcom-bubble.asp

Hayes, A. (2020, November 30). *Self-liquidating loan definition*. Investopedia. https://www.investopedia.com/terms/s/self-liquidating-loan.asp

Hayes, A. (2021, June 29). *Proof of capacity (Cryptocurrency)*. Investopedia. https://www.investopedia.com/terms/p/proof-capacity-cryptocurrency.asp

Hertig, A. (2021, July 22). *What is ether?* Coindesk. https://www.coindesk.com/learn/what-is-ether/

Hsieh, N. (2021, December 8). *New crypto tax reporting requirements in the 2021 infrastructure bill*. Volt Equity. https://www.voltequity.com/post/new-crypto-tax-reporting-requirements-in-the-2021-infrastructure-bill

Hurley, L. (2015, April 16). *7 online worlds that ended while people were still playing*. Gamesradar. https://www.gamesradar.com/7-games-shut-down-while-people-were-still-playing/

IBM. (2021). *What is blockchain technology? - IBM blockchain*. https://www.ibm.com/topics/what-is-blockchain

ICAEW. (n.d.). *History of blockchain*. https://www.icaew.com/technical/technology/blockchain-and-cryptocurrency/blockchain-articles/what-is-blockchain/history

iExec. (2022, January 25). *iExec: The decentralized marketplace for computing assets (iExec intro video 2022)* [Video]. YouTube. https://www.youtube.com/watch?v=Mkt7SY3B3Qo

Ifegwu, O. (n.d.). *Finality*. Binance Academy. https://academy.binance.com/en/glossary/finality

Iredale, G. (2020, April 14). *4 different types of blockchain technology & networks*. 101 Blockchains. https://101blockchains.com/types-of-blockchain/

IRS. (2014). *Frequently asked questions on virtual currency transactions | Internal Revenue Service*. https://www.irs.gov/individuals/international-taxpayers/frequently-asked-questions-on-virtual-currency-transactions

Ivan. (2020, August 30). *DeFi deep dive - What are decentralized marketplaces?* Moralis Academy. https://academy.moralis.io/blog/defi-deep-dive-what-are-decentralized-marketplaces

Jacquot, P. J. (2022, January 3). *iExec SDK V7*. GitHub. https://github.com/iExecBlockchainComputing/iexec-sdk

Johnes, M. (2019, March 20). *Decentralized exchange (DEX): What is it, types, DEX exchanges review*. TradeSanta. https://tradesanta.com/blog/what-is-a-decentralized-exchange

Kemmerer, D. (2022, February 11). *The comprehensive guide to DeFi taxes (2022) | CryptoTrader.Tax*. https://cryptotrader.tax/blog/defi-crypto-tax-guide

Knight, H. (2021, September 22). *Intro to Nexus Mutual: A DeFi leader In decentralized insurance*. ChainDebrief. https://chaindebrief.com/nexus-mutual-defi-leader-decentralized-insurance/

Kosinski, J. R. (n.d.). *Ethereum oracle contracts: Setup and orientation*. Toptal Engineering. https://www.toptal.com/ethereum/ethereum-oracle-contracts-tutorial-pt1.

Kotamraju, P. (2019, May 7). *What is a nonce in block chain?* Tutorials Point. https://www.tutorialspoint.com/what-is-a-nonce-in-block-chain

Lambur, H. (2021, January 15). *UMA: Crypto derivatives and universal market access*. Gemini. https://www.gemini.com/cryptopedia/uma-crypto-derivatives-market-access

Lambur, H. (2022, February 8). *UMA: Priceless contracts via data verification*. Gemini. https://www.gemini.com/cryptopedia/uma-priceless-crypto-market-access#section-token-sponsors

Laura, M. (2021, December 7). *What is a smart contract and how do smart contracts work?* BitDegree https://www.bitdegree.org/crypto/tutorials/what-is-a-smart-contract

Lightbulb Moment. (2021, December 21). *How does pool together work? DeFi savings app with daily prizes!* [Video]. YouTube https://www.youtube.com/watch?v=w0DWej97aOQ

Ma, J. (n.d.). *Latency*. Binance Academy. https://academy.binance.com/en/glossary/latency

Maher, M. (2021, September 15). *How to pay zero tax on crypto (Legally)*. YouTube. [Video] https://www.youtube.com/watch?v=PUAaAjHugiI

Malik, P. (2021, March 17). *What are smart contracts? +benefits, limitations, use cases*. The Whatfix Blog. https://whatfix.com/blog/smart-contracts-changing-legal-landscape/

Matthew, T. (2021, September 25). *Uncover the best privacy coins in 2021* HackerNoon. https://hackernoon.com/meet-the-best-privacy-coins-in-2021

McCracken, T. (2022, January 31). *Comparing FTX vs Kucoin: Which exchange is best?* Coin Bureau. https://www.coinbureau.com/review/ftx-vs-kucoin/

Mcshane, G. (2022, January 11). *What are Ethereum gas fees?* Coindesk. https://www.coindesk.com/learn/what-are-ethereum-gas-fees/

Menasakanian, J. (2021, December 21). *How will decentralised finance drive change in asset management?* Money Marketing. https://www.moneymarketing.co.uk/opinion/how-will-decentralised-finance-drive-change-in-asset-management/

Merre, R. (2021, July 31). *ICO 101 — History of initial coin offerings (ICOs)*. Medium. https://medium.com/hackernoon/ico-101-history-of-initial-coin-offerings-icos-part-1-from-mastercoin-to-ethereum-4689b7c2326b

Miracle, M. C. (2021, December 29). *How high can cardano (ADA) go?* Benzinga. https://www.benzinga.com/money/how-high-can-cardano-go/

Newman, L. H. (2021, December 24). *The worst hacks of 2021*. Wired. https://www.wired.com/story/worst-hacks-2021/

Nick. (2021, July 3). *DeFi boom: What are no-loss lotteries?* CryptosRus. https://cryptosrus.com/defi-boom-what-are-no-loss-lotteries/

O'Reilly, T. (2005). *What is Web 2.0.* Oreilly.com. https://www.oreilly.com/pub/a/web2/archive/what-is-web-20.html

O'Reilly, T. (n.d.). *Mastering Bitcoin.* Oreilly.com. https://www.oreilly.com/library/view/mastering-bitcoin/9781491902639/ch07.html

Odunayo, S. (2021, November 10). *VeChain (VET) honored as best innovation in food supply chain for 2021.* Times Tabloid. https://timestabloid.com/vechain-vet-honored-as-best-innovation-in-food-supply-chain-for-2021/

Opium.Finance. (2021, August 24). *First decentralised protection for RealT "no-occupancy" event.* https://opium.finance/blog/realt-protection/RealT/

Orcutt, M. (2018, April 25). *How secure is blockchain really?* MIT Technology Review. https://www.technologyreview.com/2018/04/25/143246/how-secure-is-blockchain-really/

Parizo, C. (2021, May 28). *What are the 4 different types of blockchain technology?* SearchCIO. https://searchcio.techtarget.com/feature/What-are-the-4-different-types-of-blockchain-technology

Pastel. (2022, January 4). *The top celebrity NFT owners.* https://pastel.network/the-top-celebrity-nft-owners/

Penn, A. (2019, October 27). *2008 bank bailout: Its true cost, and who paid it.* Shortform Books. https://www.shortform.com/blog/2008-bank-bailout/

Pham, T. T. (2018, May 18). *Exposed AWS resources leaked sensitive data.* Duo. https://duo.com/decipher/exposed-aws-resources-leaked-sensitive-data

Phung, A. (2019). *Forward contracts vs. futures contracts: What's the difference?* Investopedia.

https://www.investopedia.com/ask/answers/06/forwardsandfutures.asp

Piesse, D. (2021, September). *Decentralized finance (DeFi) – Risks and opportunities for the insurance industry*. International Insurance Society. https://www.internationalinsurance.org/Insights_decentralized_finance

Prusso, M. (2021, May 3). *All the ways to generate passive income with DeFi*. The Defiant. https://thedefiant.io/all-the-ways-to-generate-passive-income-with-defi/

R, E. (2021, December 15). *Is the crypto market heading towards another FUD crash tonight?* Coinpedia. https://coinpedia.org/news/crypto-market-heading-towards-another-fud/

Rees, K. (2022, January 11). *Web 2.0 vs. Web 3.0: What's the difference?* MUO. https://www.makeuseof.com/web-2-vs-web-3-whats-the-difference/

Reiff, N. (2021, August 24). *Why Should Anyone Invest in Crypto?* Investopedia. https://www.investopedia.com/tech/question-why-should-anyone-invest-crypto/

Richards, S. (2022, February 15). *Gas and fees*. Ethereum.org. https://ethereum.org/en/developers/docs/gas/

Rosic, A. (2017, August 21). *What is cryptoeconomics? The ultimate beginners guide*. Blockgeeks. https://blockgeeks.com/guides/what-is-cryptoeconomics/

Royal, J. (2022, February 11). *Are your lost bitcoins gone forever? Here's how you might be able to recover them*. Bankrate. https://www.bankrate.com/investing/how-to-recover-lost-bitcoins-and-other-crypto/

Russo, C. R. (2021). *What is decentralized finance?: A deep dive by the defiant*. CoinMarketCap. https://coinmarketcap.com/alexandria/article/what-is-decentralized-finance

Sharma, M. (2018, September 24). *Web 1.0, Web 2.0 and Web 3.0 with their differences.* GeeksforGeeks. https://www.geeksforgeeks.org/web-1-0-web-2-0-and-web-3-0-with-their-difference/

Shembekar, A. (2022, March 10). *What are NFTs? | How does it work & what are the business ideas for startups?* OpenXcell. https://www.openxcell.com/blog/what-are-nfts-top-5-remarkable-nft-business-ideas/

Simply Explained. (2021). *NFT's explained in 4 minutes!* [Video]. YouTube. https://www.youtube.com/watch?v=FkUn86bH34M

60 Minutes Australia. (2014, September 14). *The dark web | Silk road - Explained* [Video]. YouTube. https://www.youtube.com/watch?v=lFZLjJooBys

Simply Explained - Savjee. (2017). *How does a blockchain work? - Simply explained* [Video]. YouTube. https://www.youtube.com/watch?v=SSo_EIwHSd4

Small, Z. (2022, March 4). This time, Beeple is trying his hand at artwork for walls. *The New York Times.* https://www.nytimes.com/2022/03/04/arts/design/beeple-jack-hanley-gallery.html

Spagnolo, E. (2022, January 15). *Ethereum: Is mining no longer profitable?* The Cryptonomist. https://en.cryptonomist.ch/2022/01/15/ethereum-mining-profitable/

Staffwriter. (2022, January 20). *4 Ways to pay zero tax on cryptocurrency gains.* Escape Artist. https://www.escapeartist.com/blog/4-ways-pay-zero-tax-cryptocurrency-gains/

Sweta. (2022, January 5). *Seigniorage - Definition, latest news, and why seigniorage is important?* Cleartax. https://cleartax.in/g/terms/seigniorage

Tekeli, A. (2021, July 6). *Stablecoins explained: How they work and how they affect the lives of regular individuals.* Medium. https://medium.com/the-capital/stablecoins-explained-how-they-work-and-how-they-affect-the-lives-of-regular-individuals-3cc73faf08cf

Tether. (n.d.). *What are Tether tokens and how do they work?* https://tether.to/en/how-it-works/

The Babylonians. (2021, August 5). *InsurAce (INSUR) crypto review: How to buy DeFi insurance & earn high APY yields* [Video]. YouTube. https://www.youtube.com/watch?v=0O-bjjMdKCo

Thorbecke, C. (2021, April 14). *Coinbase goes public in "watershed event" for cryptocurrency*. ABC News. https://abcnews.go.com/Business/coinbase-set-public-watershed-event-cryptocurrency/story?id=77065101

Thurman, A. (2021, December 5). *Crypto exchange BitMart hacked with losses estimated at $196M*. Coindesk. https://www.coindesk.com/business/2021/12/05/crypto-exchange-bitmart-hacked-with-losses-estimated-at-196-million/

Vasile, I. (2021, November 22). *Coinbase vs. Robinhood: Which is better for buying crypto?* BeInCrypto. https://beincrypto.com/learn/coinbase-vs-robinhood/

Vermaak, W. (2021). *What Is Web 3.0?* CoinMarketCap. https://coinmarketcap.com/alexandria/article/what-is-web-3-0

Wade, J. (2022, January 30). *Binance vs. Coinbase: How do they compare?* The Balance. https://www.thebalance.com/binance-vs-coinbase-5118288

Walters, S. (2021, November 13). *FTX exchange review 2022: Safe exchange?? What we know!!* Coin Bureau. https://www.coinbureau.com/review/ftx-exchange/

Warwick, K. (2020, December 10). *What is Synthetix and how does it work?* Gemini. https://www.gemini.com/cryptopedia/synthetix

Watcher Guru. (2021, September 27). *A brief history of China's FUD*. Watcher Guru. https://watcher.guru/news/a-brief-history-of-china-fud

Wealth Hacker - Jeff Rose. (2021, May 20). *Bitcoin tax hack: [Legally] Avoid paying taxes on cryptocurrency* [Video]. YouTube. https://www.youtube.com/watch?v=YGoxYk3f520

Wharton University of Pennsylvania. (2021). *DEFI beyond the hype: The emerging world of decentralized finance*. Wharton University of Pennsylvania. https://wifpr.wharton.upenn.edu/wp-content/uploads/2021/05/DeFi-Beyond-the-Hype.pdf

Whiteboard Crypto. (2021a, May 9). *What are smart contracts in crypto? (4 examples + animated)* [Video]. YouTube. https://www.youtube.com/watch?v=pyaIppMhuic

Whiteboard Crypto. (2021b, May 22). *What is an automated market maker? (Liquidity pool algorithm)* [Video]. YouTube. https://www.youtube.com/watch?v=1PbZMudPP5E&t=25s

Whiteboard Crypto. (2021c, June 7). *What is yield farming in crypto? (Animated + 4 examples)* [Video]. YouTube. https://www.youtube.com/watch?v=LaeI5D6NDvw

Whiteboard Crypto. (2021d, August 3). *3 stablecoin algorithms explained (Rebase, Empty Set Dollar, Basis Cash, Iron Finance)* [Video]. YouTube. https://www.youtube.com/watch?v=S7-rfvpEpJs

Whiteboard Crypto. (2021e, October 26). *What is Web 3.0? (Explained with animations)* [Video]. YouTube. https://www.youtube.com/watch?v=nHhAEkG1y2U

Williams, R. (2019, April 23). *ICO regulations: Know which are the countries with restrictions*. Crypto Newsz. https://www.cryptonewsz.com/ico-regulations-which-are-the-countries-with-restrictions/

World Wide Web Foundation. (2018). *History of the web*. https://webfoundation.org/about/vision/history-of-the-web/

Zane, A. (2021, September 20). *IDO vs ICO - Modern finance explained*. FinanceBrokerage. https://www.financebrokerage.com/ido-vs-ico-modern-finance-explained/